THE NEXT GENERATION

THE NEXT GENERATION

The Prospects Ahead

for the Youth of Today

and Tomorrow

BY

DONALD N. MICHAEL

RANDOM HOUSE

New York

The author wishes to thank the following for permission to reprint material included in this volume:

AMERICAN ACADEMY OF ARTS AND SCIENCES—for selection from "Social Change and Youth in America," by Kenneth Keniston, in "Youth: Change and Challenge," edited by Stephen R. Graubard, in *Daedalus*, Vol. 91, No. 1, Winter, 1962; for selection from "U.S. Foreign Policy: Its Limits and Possibilities" by Stanley Hoffman in *Daedalus on the Air,* 1963; and for selection from "U.S. Foreign Policy: Its Limits and Possibilities" by Robert R. Bowie in *Daedalus on the Air,* 1963.

THE AMERICAN ACADEMY OF POLITICAL AND SOCIAL SCIENCE—for selection from "The Great Employment Controversy," by by Walter Buckingham, in "Automation," edited by Charles C. Killingsworth, *The Annals*, Vol. 340, March, 1962.

ATHENEUM PUBLISHERS—for selection from *The Public Happiness,* by August Heckscher. © Copyright 1962 by August Heckscher.

CARNEGIE CORPORATION OF NEW YORK *Quarterly*—for selection from "Education and Politics," Vol. XI, No. 1, January, 1963.

CONOVER-MAST PUBLICATIONS—for selection from "Automated Design," by Borge Langefors, in *International Science and Technology,* February, 1964.

DOUBLEDAY & COMPANY, INC.—for selection from *The Price of Prosperity,* by Peter L. Bernstein. © Copyright 1962 by The Nation Associates, Inc.; and for selection from *Prospect for America,* Rockefeller Panel Reports, © Copyright 1961 by Rockefeller Brothers Fund, Inc.

FUND FOR THE ADVANCEMENT OF EDUCATION—for selection from *Programmed Instruction Today and Tomorrow,* by Wilbur Schramm, 1962.

HARPER & ROW, INC.—for selection from *The Great Ascent* by Robert L. Heilbroner.

HARPER'S MAGAZINE—for selection from "The Next Thirty Years in the Colleges," by Christopher Jencks, October, 1961.

HEARST MAGAZINES—for selection from "What Women *Really* Think About Religion," by Richard Carter, in *Good Housekeeping,* January, 1963.

LIBERTY MUTUAL INSURANCE COMPANY FORUM—for selection from "The Post-Industrial Society," by Daniel Bell, June 14, 1962.

THE NEW REPUBLIC—for selection from "Schoolmaster Rickover," by Christopher Jencks, Vol. 148, No. 9, March 2, 1963.

JOHN WILEY & SONS, INC.—for selection from *The American College,* edited by Nevitt Sanford, 1962.

TO MY PARENTS

AND

FOR MY SON

CONTENTS

PREFACE

THIS BOOK is based on a report prepared in 1963 for the Office of the Special Assistant on Juvenile Delinquency of the Department of Health, Education, and Welfare and for other members of the President's Committee on Juvenile Delinquency and Youth Crime. The report was the result of their desire to make better known the conditions over the next twenty years that need to be considered when planning youth development programs.

The relationships discussed in this book are at once causes and effects of each other. No generally accepted conceptual model fits together events and trends so that their relationships are unique: nevertheless, both reader and author are entitled to some sort of organization which imposes order on the material. Therefore, the general arrangement of the chapters is based on these assumptions: 1) that the ultimate purpose of plans for the development of youth is to provide youth with bases for effective means of social and personal expression while they are young and when they become adults; 2) that the forms of such expression can generally be subsumed under the rubrics "work," "leisure," and "values and viewpoints"; and 3) that many factors will crucially affect youth, but that of these, only some can be influenced by those who plan and implement youth development programs. With regard to the third assumption, it should be clearly understood that this book is not an overview of *all* changes to be expected in the next twenty years. *Only those that seem especially pertinent for youth development are examined.*

The book begins with a description of those kinds of

events and circumstances that, in general, will evolve independently of youth or of those people and organizations attempting to guide youth. Section I explores developments in: 1) the general economy, 2) technology, 3) the growing rationalization of society, 4) the evolution of the urban community, 5) what may happen in the developed and underdeveloped parts of the world, 6) the opportunities for peace and war.

The second section of the book looks at trends and circumstances more within the control of the planners of youth development programs. These are: the family (and the related topics of sex and marriage) and education for all forms of expression.

The final section examines developments in modes of expression—work, leisure, and values and viewpoints—as these may be influenced by conditions speculated upon in the first two sections of the book. The first two sections, then, provide the necessary background for the third.

The book concludes with a brief summary of what the next twenty years may hold and an appendix suggesting some questions, the answers to which ought to influence youth development programs.

Most of what will be discussed in this book is not new. However, implications should not be underestimated on the grounds that "we've been faced with these problems all along and we're still in the most democratic country with the highest standard of living, etc., etc." Many of these trends and circumstances—so familiar that it is almost trite to refer to them—in stronger form, or even in their present form, will present problems and opportunities of a new order when combined with other developments.

Nor is there consistency among the trends explored

here. After all, those who will shape the next twenty years are already here, influenced by today's values, behaviors, institutions, and goals. These are not consistent; neither will be what evolves from them tomorrow.

A few words are in order about the degree of precision that should be read into expressions denoting likelihood. Repeating one phrase makes for tiresome reading. However, varying the words gives the impression that the forecasts have specific degrees of assurity assigned to them. In fact, the most that is meant to be conveyed is greater or lesser likelihood. The word "will" especially should not be understood to imply that history is assumed to be foreordained and the forecast 100 per cent likely. At its strongest, "will" is meant to suggest that a development looks like a particularly good bet. The same license holds for dates assigned to events or trends described as occurring during this next ten years or the middle 70's, and so on. The specific times are meant to give a feel for the expected pace of development; the situations faced would not seem to be much better or worse if the reader shifts the forecasts by a few years.

This book is not a scientific exercise based on consistent theory and heavily documented by field studies and laboratory research. No such theory exists for describing our society adequately—much less predicting changes in it. Aside from a few statistics about existing population characteristics, the state of formal knowledge about these matters is so small, compared to the magnitude of the circumstances examined, that it is not profitable to judge many of the speculations by the data. The data are by no means trivial, but in themselves they are seldom uniquely interpretable in terms of the range of conditions explored here. Countless numerical predictions about work force composition, economic growth, and so on, are available but all of these depend on assumptions, frequently unstated or inadequate, about the future of society. Also, they are based on extrapolations of past data, which in turn depend on special definitions of that which is measured. Determining whether or not these measures are adequate to predict the future is the sort of thing this book would hope to inspire but will not undertake. Since such figures are open to question, the report avoids specific figures whenever practicable, trying to emphasize instead the magnitudes involved. Readers wishing to evaluate these speculations in the light of other writings will find a representative bibliography at the end of each chapter.

The ideas expressed here are those of many observers of the present and speculators about the future. In particular, this book was influenced pervasively by the deliberations of seven men who contributed three intensive days and nights of their time, wisdom, and imagination to the development and refinement of their picture—and mine—of the next twenty years: Robert A. Asher, Senior Staff, Foreign Policy Studies Division, The Brookings Institution; Daniel Bell, Professor and Chairman, Department of Sociology, Columbia College, Columbia University; George Boehm, Science Editor, *Fortune* Magazine; David Riesman, Henry Ford II Professor of Social Sciences, Harvard University; Herbert Striner, Director of Program Development, the W. E. Upjohn Institute for Employment Research; Robert Theobald, consultant on economics and technology, New York City; and Stephen Withey, Professor of Psychology and Research Program Director at the Institute for Social Research, University of Michigan. All are distinguished for their disciplined imagination and their wide-ranging

familiarity and concern with society in general. Some
are also experts on youth, youth culture, or youth development. With the exception of Robert Asher, they all
read, criticized, and helped to extend the first draft of
the report.

In the process of planning the study, many people
gave of their time and experience to provide criticism,
insight, and candid suggestions about what they and I
foresaw as trends and developments. In particular, I
would express my thanks to Leon Greenberg, Assistant
Commissioner for Productivity and Technological Development, Bureau of Labor Statistics, U.S. Department
of Labor; Sterling McMurrin, then U.S. Commissioner
of Education; Wilfred Owen, Senior Staff, Economics
Study Division, The Brookings Institution; Herbert Sal-
inger, Special Assistant to the Secretary of Labor in
Youth Matters; Ben Seligman, Director of Education
and Research of the Retail Clerks International Association; Eugene Skolnikoff, then of the President's Advisory
Committee on Science and Technology; Edgar Wein-
berg, Chief, Branch of Technological Studies, Bureau
of Labor Statistics, U.S. Department of Labor; and
Edward Wenk, Technical Specialist, Office of Science
and Technology.

Drafts of the report were read, in part or in full, by
Isaac Asimov, Associate Professor of Biochemistry, Boston University School of Medicine; Raymond Bauer,
Professor, Harvard Business School; Charles Bowen,
Manager of Education Products, IBM Corporation; An-
tonia Chayes, then Technical Secretary to the Committee
on Education, the President's Commission on the Status
of Women; Charles de Carlo, Director of Education,
IBM Corporation; Peter Drucker, Professor of Management and Area Chairman of the Graduate School of

Business Administration, New York University; Dr. Leonard J. Duhl, Psychiatrist, Professional Services Branch, National Institute of Mental Health; Todd Gitlin, Senior, Harvard University; Nathan Glazer, then Director, Office of Program Policy, Housing and Home Finance Agency; Morton Grodzins, Professor, Department of Political Science, University of Chicago; Robert Heilbroner, Economist, New School for Social Research; Christopher Jencks, Associate Editor, *The New Republic;* Edward Katzenbach, Jr., Deputy Assistant Secretary of Defense for Education, U.S. Department of Defense; Eric Larrabee, Managing Editor, *Horizon;* Harold Lasswell, Professor, Yale University Law School; Erich Lindeman, Psychiatrist-in-Chief, Massachusetts General Hospital; Seymour M. Lipset, Director, Institute of International Studies, University of California; Carol McEldowney, Research Assistant, Peace Research Institute; Kenneth McEldowney, then Manpower Development Specialist, Office of Manpower, Automation, and Training, U.S. Department of Labor; Richard L. Meier, Professor, Department of Conservation, School of Natural Resources, University of Michigan; Rhoda Metraux, Associate Director, Project on the Factor of Allopsychic Orientation in Mental Health, American Museum of Natural History; Marcus Raskin, then Member of the National Security Council White House Staff; Henry Riecken, Assistant Director for Social Sciences, National Science Foundation; Gus Tyler, then Director of Departments of Politics, Education, and Training, International Ladies' Garment Workers' Union; Arthur Waskow, Senior Staff, Peace Research Institute; Charles Willie, Research Director, Washington Project, President's Committee on Juvenile Delinquency and Youth Crime; and Christopher Wright, Executive Director,

Council for Atomic Age Studies, Columbia University. Their criticisms, suggestions, and encouragement have added enormously to the substance, balance, and spirit of this book and I am very much indebted to them for taking time to give ideas and criticisms in the middle of their own busy lives.

Special thanks for help and support are due those directly involved with the President's Committee and the HEW office who arranged a grant through the Committee to the Peace Research Institute (now part of the Institute for Policy Studies) to support the study. They gave ideas, and moral support throughout: Richard Boone, then Director, Program Development Section, U.S. Justice Department; Hyman Frankel, then Training Coordinator, Office of the Special Assistant, U.S. Department of Health, Education, and Welfare; Lloyd Ohlin, then Director, President's Committee on Juvenile Delinquency and Youth Crime; and Bernard Russell, Special Assistant to the Secretary of Health, Education, and Welfare.

Velma Doby, Laura McConnell, and Carol McEldowney gave endless efficient and good-natured help during the study and in the preparation of the report. Carolyn McKnight Nichols' administrative ability relieved me of many burdens which, if I had had them, never would have been carried out with her efficiency and graciousness. And Patricia McMonigle was responsible for most of the editing necessary to transform the report into a book and for overseeing related administrative matters. Her style and spirit, in large part, carried the manuscript and author, respectively, through this trying period.

To all, the author expresses his deepest appreciation; to the core of seven, his beholden acknowledgment that the original report would not have been done without their vigorous involvement.

My wife Margot has played a very special role in all this. As confidante, homemaker, and especially as the mother-planner of our young son's development, she has helped me as no one else could to stay in touch with the human reality that is too easily lost in abstract speculation on the future.

The final responsibility for the book must be the author's, for the ideas he has been graciously or cantankerously offered by others have been screened, extrapolated, embellished, played one against the other, and added to as his own understanding—and biases—have inclined him. Although the report has been edited in the interests of readability, none of its substance has been changed. Nor, with the exception of a few references, has it been updated since its completion in May 1963: nothing that has happened since then has changed my mind about the developments and trends examined herein—"wars" on poverty and women in high government office notwithstanding.

PREVIEW:
Twenty Years of People

. . . In July 1964, the population of the United States was about 192 million people. The U.S. Census Bureau estimates that the population in 1975 will be between 226 and 235 million, and that in 1980 it will be between 246 and 260 million.

. . . World population was over 3 billion in 1964. If fertility remains at present levels until 1975 and then begins to decline, the population of the world will reach 4 billion in 1977, 5 billion by about 1990.

. . . In 1973, those who are now infants or young children will be in late primary school or early high school. Those now in the eighth grade will be marrying, competing for work, or in college. By 1983, their children will be well into primary school. In 1973, most of those now entering the work force or finishing college will be through with childbearing and infant raising, and many of these women will be ready to re-enter the work force. Their children will be in primary school and high school. Those now in their 40's and 50's will be retiring or getting ready to. In 1983, those who are now infants will be ready for the work force or in college. Those now entering the work force will be middle-aged and their children will be in high school, or college, or competing for jobs. Those now middle-aged will be retired.

FOREWORD

IF, over the next two decades, we are to have adequate planning for the development of the youth of this country, it is mandatory that those carrying these responsibilities have some comprehension of the kind of world they and young people will be moving into. The primary purpose of this book is to draw attention to trends and circumstances over the next twenty years that ought to be considered when planning for youth development— whether the task is to encourage well-to-do adolescent females to seek careers in engineering or to inculcate self-respect in a child alienated from society through color and poverty, whether the planner is a parent or a public welfare agency.

In this world, predicting what *will* happen is often impossible, but it is possible to sense likely developments, and to recognize developments which, if they do materialize, will have especially profound consequences. Just as we try to anticipate and plan for the defense of the nation under important, if improbable, situations, so too must we be able to plan for the development of youth in the face of alternative circumstances. We cannot afford to base these plans on a single set of assumptions about the future; certainly, we cannot base them upon optimistic assumptions simply because these are the pleasantest and easiest to cope with within prevailing institutions, resources, and agendas. Therefore, we shall explore developments differing in degree of likelihood which, if they *do* come about, will be exceedingly important for youth.

Although all recent years have been transition periods, the next twenty will be especially influenced by crucial unknowns, and social and technological developments that could not have been predicted may vitiate what is forecast here. Most important is whether there will continue to be a complex society in the Northern Hemisphere or whether, some time before the 1980's, nuclear war will have abolished future problems and opportunities alike. The discussion that follows is based on the splendidly important premise that either there will be sensible and successful attempts to preserve our future through varying degrees of arms control and disarmament, or we will be blessed with miraculous good luck.

This is an ironic way to begin a report on the world in which the youth of the future will live, but an ironic and tentative world is the one youth will live in, if they live at all, and those who would plan for their development can only plan well if they themselves are aware of the irony and the tentativeness.

Both attractive and unattractive developments are anticipated herein. Perhaps the reader will be inclined to doubt that this or that anticipated unpleasant trend or circumstance will come about because something will surely be done to block or redirect it—a move that is, of course, possible and in some cases probable. I obviously share this hope, since a major aim of the book is to imply where action will be needed in order that opportunities may be embraced and problems avoided. But it hardly has to be pointed out that many aspects of our society have been in sore need of revision for a long time. Endless reports and recommendations have already identified at least some of the crucial problems. Although, in principle, revisions could be accomplished by government or private action, they either are not made or are made slowly or inadequately. This is inherent in a pluralistic society with its diverse time perspectives, political pressures, and values. It is also in the nature of complex societies that total, over-all actions are exceedingly difficult to engineer and that partial actions may be neutralized by uncontrolled activities in other sectors. Although solutions might be worked out for a given problem, the uneasy interdependence of the parts of our society makes it very doubtful that all the consequences of the initial action will be salutary. Institutions with different goals and priorities have a hard time finding a common denominator sufficiently compelling and sufficiently potent to inspire them to work together with sincere commitment to a truly significant program. Moreover, one problem's meat may be another problem's poison. Especially (but certainly not exclusively) in a democracy, it is difficult to implement one favored program without generating obstructions to it.

Of course, the Congress or the Supreme Court, even without the leadership of a great President, could rise to the persistent needs of the society and initiate or sustain a sequence of interlocking laws and measures that might meet some of the basic problems and take advantage of some of the great opportunities described in this book. They might, but it is more likely that the Supreme Court will be the same sort of agent for change or stasis it is today, given its role, its composition as determined by the processes of selection, and its uneasy relations with the legislative branch. And most observers despair that anything will make Congress a truly effective agency short of radical changes yet to be agreed on (1).* Social crises could produce some changes, but might destroy our democratic processes altogether. I am

* Parenthetical numbers are to references at the ends of chapters.

sure that we will experience these crises, possibly even disasters, but what effects they will have directly and indirectly on the conduct of government cannot be predicted. Probably we will not experience such a total crisis or profound social disaster as to result in the radical alteration of Congress or the Court. Instead, we are likely to bumble along, using crises that arise as bases for partial institution change. Such changes may deal with one part of a problem but hardly with the tangled relationships that characterize both the threat and opportunity inherent in complex, technologically based societies. Moreover, in the nature of crisis-induced changes, it is unlikely that wisdom will dominate or that, if it could, it would have the needed answers or the persistence or power to see them through.

Another very important reason for the slowness of reform or revision is that interpretations differ as to the *nature* of the present state of affairs. Even when there is concurrence on what the state of affairs is, there are profound disagreements on the reasons for it. Laymen disagree with "experts" and both disagree among themselves. These disagreements lead to different expectations about the future, and hence to different opinions about the requirement for and type of action needed.

In summary, as a 1961 Rockefeller Panel Report put it:

To get changes recognized, to inject new facts into the political process, are recognized tasks of statesmanship. At present these tasks are formidable. Policies lag behind awareness; awareness lags behind the constantly evolving reality. Even responsible leaders find it hard to adjust their minds to the existing, but rapidly passing, state of things. The public at large, disturbed by recurrent crises, often indifferent or poorly informed, thinks in terms of the past decade or even century—when any one year brings changes enough to require a review of policy. As a result, the image of the world existing in the public mind is often strangely unreal. Lacking a secure footing in reality, men tend to project themselves into a nonexistent future or else into an irretrievable past. (2)

Detailed observational and numerical data and systematic research could help to resolve conflicting hypotheses or views about the facts and causes of given circumstances. The techniques of the behavioral sciences, economics, and related disciplines—even with their present limitations—could provide far more information and understanding than we ask of them. Indeed, out of vested interests, blind ignorance, and egregious commitment to our personal ways of evaluating the world, we do not effectively use the data and methods that already exist. This book will have served well if it succeeds in stimulating needed study, data collection, and the wise and imaginative application of what is learned.

There were, to my mind, good reasons for writing this book in emotionally neutral prose. In the first place, the subject is complicated enough without adding to it my estimate of the moral or ethical implications of what appears to be in store for youth or my delight or despair about it. In the second place, the book is intended to be read as a background paper, as a kind of social Rorschach into which the reader can project his own emotions and from which he might be inspired to action.

Let me be perfectly clear, however, about my own feelings. I welcome some of the coming changes, such as those which help to increase the opportunities for more meaningful lives for a relatively larger proportion of people. But as a father, as a nature lover, and as one who would like to see the traditional goals of democracy better realized, I don't, by and large, like the general trend

I see coming. As a social scientist I have to acknowledge that some of what distresses me personally probably will be all right for those adapted to it; other things I don't think will be at all all right, adapted or otherwise. Nevertheless, this book is itself one expression of my hopes and concerns about the future; I trust it will also help readers to better examine their own.

References

1. Cater, Douglass, *Power in Washington.* New York: Random House, Inc., 1964.

2. *Rockefeller Panel Reports,* Prospect for America. New York: Doubleday & Company, Inc., 1961, p. 6.

Supplementary Reference

Collins, LeRoy, Orville L. Freeman, Hubert H. Humphrey, Newton B. Minow, Hyman G. Rickover, and Thurgood Marshall, *The Mazes of Modern Government: The States, the Legislature, the Bureaucracy, the Courts.* Santa Barbara, Calif.: Center for the Study of Democratic Institutions, 1963.

SECTION

I

*Conditions Essentially
Independent of the Influence of
Youth Developers*

C H A P T E R

1

THE ECONOMY

OVER the next two decades the characteristics of the American economy will be especially important for youth. More than ever before, the American economy will very likely be responsive to extra-national economic pressures; changing rapidly under the impact of new technologies, new social problems and new opportunities; diminishing its independent businesses as they are bought up by industrial giants intent on reducing competition and finding new investments; envolving new working arrangements between government and private enterprise. For the most part, the economy will operate in ways beyond the control of youth planners. However, the influx of youth into the market, as both producers and consumers, will be much greater than ever before—26 million more by 1970—entering the labor force in the late 60's at the rate of one million more a year than now. This factor seems likely to influence the economy significantly.

Since the economy is so sensitive to political considerations and the timing of government decisions, it is especially difficult to anticipate trends and circumstances in this area. This chapter is meant chiefly to convey a general sense of plausible and significant economic trends and developments. The implications of many aspects of the economy are explored in other sections of this book.

I assume here, and throughout this book, that a continuing tension will exist between people driving toward a more highly rationalized society and others who are committed to making do, to self-interested "free enterprise" in business, politics, and the search for knowledge. While it is reasonable to expect the government to take more actions to head off or accelerate anticipated economic developments, still, for many important alterations of economic and social policy, it will take the fact of crisis to begin to resolve the long-continuing deadlock between the Congressional political parties and the Executive political parties, elucidated by Professor James McGregor Burns. (1)

PRODUCTIVITY AND CONSUMPTION

U.S. productivity will probably continue to increase at least at the present rate of GNP growth, if not more. Even at modest rates of increase, and allowing for population growth and considerable increases in government spending and private investment in capital goods, over-all consumption will have to increase substantially if this greater productivity is to be absorbed sufficiently to keep our economy working reasonably well. According to the economist Peter L. Bernstein:

Unless the demand for goods and services expands at least as rapidly as the 3.8 percent a year rate that prevailed during 1947-57 when pent-up demand and savings were both very great, we shall have a serious burden of unemployment even if GNP per man-hour only increases at the average rate of 2.3 percent achieved over the period from 1900 to 1957. (2)

As overproduction becomes more pressing, so, too, will drives to emphasize other kinds of consumption and to invent new products to consume. In particular, pressure for consumption in the areas of public welfare will increase.

In this century, the automobile and TV were two technological developments which have given enormous impetus to the economy, and they will doubtless continue to be important. But there is no good evidence that any new product now in its developmental and testing phase holds within it the seeds of an additional huge private consumer market—not for the next several years, at least. Gains in jobs and consumption related to services, particularly in recreation, could accelerate the economy, but these developments are subject to the usual variety of factors influencing rate of growth and output and consumption of that output. Urban renewal and construction and housing in general —especially the construction of new cities and towns —could be enormous accelerators to the economy; estimates for the costs of a really adequate program of urban renewal run between three and twelve billion dollars a year. (3) Such a level of urban renewal would require planning and investment on a scale that only the government can provide. But, since many critical political issues would be involved, it is unlikely that the government can, in the absence of an economic or social crisis, move quickly in this area or on the scale required. On the other hand, building new cities may become a very attractive investment for the huge and growing pools of uncommitted funds in banks, insurance companies, and industry—especially if the government encourages the aerospace firms, through research and development subsidies, to invade the building industry. (Such a market might fully use the management, engineering, and production resources of the aerospace industry, thereby compensating it for the loss of defense research and development which would occur—indeed, is occurring—in a more arms-controlled world.)

In the next two decades foreign-made products, especially European, Russian, and Japanese, will increasingly compete with ours in quality and quantity both here and abroad. This will be especially true as these countries resort more to automation and computer-planned economic policies, including bloc-trading and market selection. Already, these changes are beginning as European investors find their profit squeezed between increased wages and tough competition. (4) There is good evidence that the USSR is beginning to plan its trade strategies in similar ways. (5, 6) To meet this competition American business will have to place greater stress on efficiency. High American labor costs and tax write-offs, encouraging investment in new equipment, can only lead to greater application of automation and computers.

The competitive impact of European trade has a further implication:

The Common Market is the means of bringing together a number of smaller entities into one major trading confederation. This confederation will then be in a position to exact increasingly stringent terms of trade from those nations or other trading groups outside of itself. This has major import with respect to the effectiveness of a U.S. commercial policy and the use of this commercial policy to gain economic and political ends. Inevitably, the United States standing alone must increasingly lose its ability to affect the commercial policies of the Common Market nations because the United States will be dealing less and less with individual nations where it can exert appropriate economic and political leverage and increasingly with one large economic trading unit, the Common Market. (7)

Then, too, according to the authoritative Conference on Economic Progress, in 1960 there were 34 million people with family incomes totaling less than $4000 a year, and four million unattached people with incomes of less than $2000 a year. Another 37 million had deprivation-level family incomes of less than $6000 a year, and two million unattached individuals in this category were living on less than $3000 a year. (8) In this economic group, the problems of the aged will present society with increasing political and ethical pressures. In 1962, about half of those over sixty-five living alone had incomes of less than $1100. Of close to seven million families with head of family over sixty-five, half had annual incomes of less than $2800. (9) As those able to meet the professional, technological, and skilled service needs of the country receive higher salaries, the gap between the well-to-do and the poor may well widen faster than it already has. The situation will be further complicated by a disproportionately large portion of the unskilled, and of those unemployed because they are unskilled, who will be Negro.

Thus, if there is inadequate planning and action, especially for the poor, the increase in per capita consumption needed to absorb new productivity will be difficult to attain. If efforts are lacking, or if they fail to solve the present situation, later in this decade a large proportion of unskilled workers under twenty-five and at least the older female portion of the work force will have low incomes or none at all as technological changes eliminate their job possibilities.

To help meet the very serious situation of too few

skilled workers and too many unskilled without work, training and retraining very probably will be practiced on an ever larger scale. It will have to be encouraged and directed where necessary with government funds and organization, and undertaken independently by industry and unions. But training and retraining will not remove all the major employment and disemployment (not hired, as contrasted to fired) problems the nation will face in the next decade. Many of those who will need better-paying jobs will not have the underlying ability and/or experience in thinking, motivation, and learning to learn to be trained for a task that pays reasonably well, and the research and development needed to discover how to overcome these deficiencies will take years.

Increasing amounts of pertinent and detailed data on the state of the labor force and on patterns and levels of consumption; organized political pressure, in part stimulated by the implications of these data; increasing pressures both at home and abroad to enhance our humanitarian image; increasing requirements for an already high-consuming society to absorb its automated output —all will encourage, indeed push, the invention of arrangements allowing economically and humanely adequate consumption by those who cannot earn enough through their own efforts. There will be more and more talk about providing individual subsidies—perhaps money, perhaps free services. When the talk becomes action, the extent to which the subsidies will either be direct or provided through work on government-subsidized social welfare projects will, to an extent, depend on the political consequences of stressing one rather than the other. Probably both methods will be used. (10)

There is another side, too, to the relation of skills to

the condition and conduct of the economy. The recognized need for professionals will increase enormously in the next twenty years as our social welfare requirements become critical. As far ahead as we can see, there will be shortages of high-quality professional and semiprofessional manpower. The educational system cannot train them in the numbers needed, and there are no signs of spectacular increase in the number of youths choosing such careers.

The inevitable result will be that, one way or another, highly skilled personnel will be more selectively and rigorously used. Major investments of national resources will be committed or denied more and more in terms of the over-all implications for the society, in terms of the degree to which the potential investment subtracts from or adds to the social utility of the skilled manpower involved. Business, government, and the military will all have to deal with this difficulty; how it will be resolved in detail is unclear, but it is perfectly clear that not all favorite projects and programs will be pursued, no matter what their importance for the particular proponents. The economy then will be increasingly subject to a kind of welfare bookkeeping, in which the efficient use of skilled manpower will be more and more a fundamental measure of social profit and loss.

If, during this period, significant cutbacks are made in armaments—and this development is not at all unlikely—the economy will have to make major adjustments. Economists who have studied the matter believe substantial arms reductions can be made without threatening the long-range state of the economy; in fact, such reductions might well improve its over-all condition (by, for example, increasing the attention given to and economic incentives for all-out urban renewal). But they also point out that some firms and regions of the country would have to shift activities and personnel, and that much advanced planning by government and industry and much government participation during the transition would be necessary to ease the readjustment. (11) Changes in products, use of manpower, population concentrations (with all that this means for Congressmen whose districts represent a concentration of arms industry workers), as well as new sources and subjects for government funds for research, development, and production, would result in much turmoil in top management circles. Certainly, this would be as threatening and exhilarating a period for financers and managements as for workers.

UNIONS

What about unions over the next twenty years? A renaissance of unionism as a social movement seems very unlikely. Differing political and economic interests in the internal structures of the unions, their differing relations to other major social factors, and the transformations in society discussed herein preclude the resurgence of a monolithic socialist ideology of social change as it existed in the past. The unions as institutions will respond to the same types of social pressures and opportunities as other large institutions.

Even a deep depression would not be likely to lead to a repetition of the older pattern, since other forces moving the society would be quite different from those of the past. As the number of unskilled disemployed and unemployed increases, the unions could try to organize them, but this doesn't seem likely since there is nothing much to organize them for; their economic value will be negative. However, it is likely that the unions will, through their leadership, add social pressure to that of other institutions seeking to move government and business to improve the lot of these people.

The unions will pursue their traditional function of increasing and maintaining gains in economic and working conditions on the job. Nevertheless, under the impact of automation and other technological changes, many unions are losing membership, and this trend probably will not be reversed. Indeed, over-all membership loss may be accelerated if unions press—as they probably will—for shorter hours to spread the work. Since this would, in effect, increase man-hour costs it would be a further incentive to use automatic machines.

Further efforts will very likely be made to organize service and white-collar workers, especially those with relatively unskilled jobs. The unionized white-collar groups will grow, but they are unlikely to expand with anything like the vigor of the old blue-collar organizational period. By and large, these unions will serve to forward social, rather than predominantly economic, needs in working environments that are becoming more rationalized and depersonalized. To the extent that they obtain better and more secure working conditions for their members, they will in many cases simply accelerate the replacement of humans by machines. And too, there almost certainly will be a very large pool of unskilled unemployed willing to work for less than union wages. Others not replaceable by machines, such as good teachers, secretaries, and engineers, could be unionized, but many of them are already at least partial beneficiaries of the fringe-benefit system of paid medical care, continuing education, insurance, and so on. Although their lot could be better, they will not, as a group, be so deprived as to be full of the zeal for unionization that characterized workers of an earlier day. The general rise in the standard of living of the usefully skilled, and the expectation that this rise will continue, will certainly not encourage a desire to be unionized. The ambivalent attitude of liberals toward unions, reinforced by recent congressional investigations, the general anti-boat-rocking state of mind of the middle class, plus the traditional reluctance of the white-collar class to be organized or to be affiliated with what customarily has been chiefly a blue-collar activity, will make it very difficult for the unions to inspire white-collar affiliation. Again, unions formed from such groups are likely to be primarily social organizations providing group identity for members, and sometimes, opportunities for serving other needs of society through union organizations.

By and large, the unions have been reluctant to admit to leadership those who have not come up through the ranks. (12) In recent years many unions have been preoccupied with protecting the jobs and futures of their older members, often by restricting new entries and new ideas. It is not likely that the old guard will or can change its perspective rapidly and imaginatively enough to capture the interest of a younger generation that could add new drive and new viewpoints to the movement. The new generation of leadership that will replace the present one in a few years seems to share the perspectives of the one it will replace. Changing the views and goals of leadership through the efforts of staff researchers and policy proposers will be slow, for the most part, because of this up-from-the-ranks tradition.

Another trend, analogous to the routinization of entrepreneurship in large businesses, will affect the unions.

Pressures for representation of the public in management–labor disputes, plus the increasing interlocking of social processes, will encourage unions to work in rationalized contexts more than they have in the past. Sometimes, as is already the case, management and unions will make common cause; sometimes they will differ. But growing government and public pressures will restrain union independence and the enthusiasm of leadership within particular unions for politically inexpedient actions.

Changing job categories and work environments— especially those that make the worker part of an automated system rather than a discrete contributor to production—will make it more difficult to build unions around easily identifiable and distinguishable sets of crafts or industries. The resulting conflicts of interest among and within unions, the diffusion of functional identification, will not increase the monolithic strength of any union or group of unions.

All in all, it is likely that the future of the unions as a vigorous force for economic reform, based on the leverage of denying access to economically valuable people until the reforms are made, will not be great. More likely, the unions will persist as a pressure bloc for some social reforms, speaking out for and participating in better vocational schooling, welfare support, better leisure-time facilities, and so on. In Walter Reuther's words:

It was inevitable in the early days of unionism, since there was so much to be done in the matter of improving living and working standards, that the labor movement would be devoted almost exclusively to those things. In its next phase, . . . these things will be de-emphasized—not neglected— and the unions will take on the broader function of concern for the quality of our society as a whole. The labor movement will become less of an economic movement and more of a social movement. It will be concerned with the economic factors, of course, but also with the moral, the spiritual, the intellectual, and the social nature of our society, and all of this in terms of an ultimate objective—the fulfillment of the complete human being. (13)

References

1. Burns, James MacGregor, *The Deadlock of Democracy.* Englewood Cliffs, N.J.: Prentice-Hall, 1963.

2. Bernstein, Peter L., *The Price of Prosperity.* New York: Doubleday & Company, Inc., 1962, p. 113.

3. Dyckman, John W., and Reginald Isaacs, with the assistance of Peter R. Senn, *Action: Capital Requirements for Urban Development and Renewal.* New York: McGraw-Hill Book Co., 1961, p. 202.

4. Dale, Edwin L., "Cloud Dominates European Scene—Fears Voiced that Boom is Losing Steam—Wages Rise More Than Production," Special to the New York Sunday *Times* from Paris, Financial Section (3), October 14, 1962.

5. "Soviet Computer Plans Economy: Machine Calculates Data for 435 Production Sectors," New York *Times,* April 14, 1963, p. 32.

6. Berg, A. I., Adm., *Cybernetics at the Service of Communism:* Vol. I. Joint Publications Research Service, U. S. Department of Commerce, Report #JPRS, July 25, 1962.

7. *National Economic Effectiveness: The Role of U. S. Foreign Economic Policy in World Conflict.* Menlo Park, California: Stanford Research Institute Project 3711, February 1962, (Prepared for the Office of the Director, Office of Emergency Planning, Washington, D.C.), p. 59.

8. *Poverty and Deprivation in the United States,* Conference on Economic Progress, Washington, D.C., April 1962.

9. *Current Population Reports,* Series P-60, No. 37, Consumer Income Table 4, U. S. Department of Commerce, Washington, D.C., January 1962.

10. Theobald, Robert, "Abundance, Threat or Promise?" *Nation,* Vol. 196, No. 19, May 11, 1963, p. 387.

11. Benoit, Emile, *et al., Economic Impacts of Disarmament,* United States Arms Control and Disarmament Agency Pamphlet No. 2, Series 1, Washington, D.C.: U. S. Government Printing Office, January 1962.

12. Solomon, M. I., "Youth—Challenge to Labor," *Labor Today*, Introductory No. 2, Fall 1962, p. 39.

13. McDonald, Donald, "The Corporation and the Union," The *American Character Series*. Santa Barbara, Calif.: Center for the Study of Democratic Institutions, 1962.

Supplementary References

American Academy of Political and Social Science, *The Annals*, Volume 340, March 1962, Special Edition on "Automation," Charles C. Killingsworth, ed., Philadelphia, 1962.

Bator, Francis M., "The Uses of Economics, Panel Comments," Chapter IV in *Research for Public Policy: Brookings Dedication Lectures*. Washington, D.C.: Brookings Institution, March 1961.

Bazelon, David T., *The Paper Economy*. New York: Random House, Inc., 1962.

Berle, Adolf A., *The American Economic Republic*. New York: Harcourt, Brace & World, 1963.

Burbash, Jack, *Labor's Grass Roots: A Study of the Local Union*. University of California Press, 1959.

Ferry, W. H., "Caught on the Horn of Plenty." Santa Barbara, Calif.: Center for the Study of Democratic Institutions, January 1962.

Harrington, Michael and Paul Jacobs, *Labor in a Free Society*. New York: Harper & Row, 1961.

Hitch, Charles J., "The Uses of Economics," in *Research for Public Policy: Brookings Dedication Lectures*. Washington, D.C.: Brookings Institution, March 1961, p. 91.

Kolko, Gabriel, *Wealth and Power in America*. New York: Praeger, 1962.

Lens, Sidney, *Crisis of American Labor*. New York: A. S. Barnes, 1961.

Lester, Richard, *As Unions Mature*. Princeton, N.J.: Princeton University Press, 1958.

Lipset, Seymour Martin, "The Political Process in Trade-Unions," in *Political Man*. New York: Doubleday & Company, Inc., 1959, 1960.

MacDonald, Dwight, "Our Invisible Poor," *The New Yorker*, XXXVIII, No. 48, January 19, 1963.

Orbach, Harold L., and Clark Tibbitts, eds., *Aging and the Economy*. Ann Arbor: University of Michigan Press, 1963.

Theobald, Robert, *The Challenge of Abundance*. New York: Clarkson N. Potter, Inc., 1961.

United States Arms Control and Disarmament Agency, *The Economic and Social Consequences of Disarmament*, Part II, Economic Series 2. Washington, D.C.: U. S. Government Printing Office, March 1962.

CHAPTER

2

TECHNOLOGICAL DEVELOPMENTS

INTRODUCTION

THIS SOCIETY has chosen to emphasize technological change as its chief mode of creative expression and basis for economic growth. If the growth in recent years of investment in research and development is any indicator, the future should show at least as much technological innovation as the past. Whether the changes are in fact introduced, and what effects they have on society, will depend on many factors in addition to the intrinsic assets of these innovations.

Of special importance, the consumption of trained manpower and the enormous costs of developing some technologies will be so great that national and private investments in new technologies will become increasingly selective and preclusive. There will not be enough good scientists and engineers or enough politically approved dollars to pursue all the interesting extensions and applications of knowledge promoted by different and differing groups of scientists, engineers, entrepreneurs, politicians, and statesmen. In order to advance some types of progress there will be growing control and sometimes inhibition of scientific and technological efforts in areas deemed of lesser priority. (1) To be sure, this is already true to some extent—myths about being unable to stop science (and technology) notwithstanding. Such inhibition will become a much more deliberate policy in the future, and will be much more evident too, given the growing power and publicity of competing science and technology lobbies.

The significance of new technological developments for youth resides in two general implications. First, careers and occupations will be profoundly affected. In particular, the growing tendency for the government to stimulate and support major technological developments, and the susceptibility of that support to changing priorities, means that many engineers, technicians, and scientists will have to be prepared to shift topics of interest and accept variations in income as programs are expanded or contracted. This is especially likely to be true in large research and development areas. As other technologies are expanded, the status and intellectual attractiveness of new areas will compete with those that are now the most glamorous. All in all, professional updating and change of employer will be frequent for many engineers, technicians, and scientists. Such shifts in emphasis will also tend to be reflected—often inadequately—in education for occupations.

For youth the other major implication of changing technology will be its effect on their values and attitudes. These and other implications are examined in other parts of this book. (In particular, this chapter will not describe, much less explore, the social and ethical issues raised by social engineering, hallucinogenic agents, oral contraceptives, and so on.) This chapter is intended only to provide a sense of what technological developments are plausible over the next twenty years.

The technological changes or developments selected for emphasis in this report are those which now appear to be: (a) technologically plausible or feasible in the next two decades in the light of *present* scientific knowledge or preliminary research and development efforts; and (b) likely to have important social implications pertinent for youth either by accelerating present trends or engendering new problems and opportunities for society, while still being sufficiently compatible with prevailing circumstances to make it likely that they will be embraced rather than rejected, once they become available.

Most innovations will not have significant implications for the conduct or directions of society, either here or abroad; for the most part they will simply let us do better or by different means things already being done, without significantly changing the social context thereby (though they may provide new jobs and incentives for consumption). Such innovations are not discussed here. The developments highlighted are doubtless not the only ones that should be considered, nor is it likely that all will come to fruition or have important social consequences. Certainly, the degree of development and application of technology will be strongly influenced by the general state of the economy. Given the enormous growth in working-age population in the next two decades, the rate and types of technological development will be especially influenced by the relationships between number of unemployed, productivity increases, and wage levels. (2)

CYBERNATION

The application of automation and computers (cyber-nation) to an ever greater variety of tasks is expected to increase rapidly. The requirements for low-cost production, particularly under pressures from foreign competition, and the strong tendency to deal with unemployment and a slow rate of increase in GNP by increasing consumption at home, will encourage the use of automatic, and thereby relatively inexpensive, production of material objects. And only the enormous capabilities of computers will provide decision-makers with the bases for sufficient understanding fast enough to anticipate, plan for, and cope with the social complexity produced by population growth, technological change itself, and the social and welfare services needed to meet these changes.

As well as mass, continuous-flow production, general-purpose automation will permit short runs of specialized production. In many situations, operating economies and social changes, in part induced by the requirements for efficient operation of cybernated systems, will result in around-the-clock operation of the system. Cybernated facilities will be applied to a growing variety of service industries, too, especially industries serving large numbers of people (e.g., banks and supermarkets). (3) Cybernated equipment with very long, reliable life-times will be partially the result of cybernated fabrication and maintenance methods. As a result, components will often be more economical to replace than to repair. In general, automation, miniaturization, and special-purpose materials will result in more fabrication of electrical and mechanical devices that are modular and non-repairable.

Improvements in multipurpose computers and their programing, including the development of central libraries of computer programs and computer data and of computers that can do much of their own programing, will add to the incentive to apply them. These resources will increase the number of computer users who are not expert in computer design or programing. Centralized computer facilities simultaneously serving many small organizations (via telephone and teletype) will provide some advantages accruing to large organizations which can afford their own computers and computer personnel. Pushed by the pressures of the "information explosion," language translation by computers will improve and be applied on a larger scale, especially to technical and professional literature. Data reduction and literature searching, abstracting, and cross-referencing will increasingly be done by computers.

SOCIAL ENGINEERING

Improvements, modest to substantial, can be expected in predicting and influencing the behavior of individuals and groups and in screening and selection methods. Systematic knowledge will increase about individual motivation, thought, and the processes of learning, as well as about group and institutional behavior. A major tool in the advancement of this knowledge will be the computer programed to simulate individual and institutional behavior. The results will be compared with actual behavior and, in this way, theories describing individual and group behavior will be refined. These scientific developments, stimulated by the need for better measures of social costs and social value, will result in practical joint economic-behavioral science models of social processes. The ethical issues regarding their use will grow apace.

Experiments in and applications of technology that supplements or replaces the human teacher will increase. These will include audio-visual aids, especially closed- and open-circuit television and movies. Simple teaching machines, augmented by programed instruction materials, especially for subjects whose mastery requires rote learning of facts and methods, will be increasingly used. So will elaborate teaching machines that simulate the environment in which the subject being learned is to be used. Some of these machines will provide a "responsive environment" that automatically rewards the student for correct responses, and feeds him material to be learned at a rate and complexity determined by his previous rate and quality of success. (4)

At some time during this period it is highly likely that experimental programs will be undertaken to augment the capacity to learn through chemicals which stimulate alertness, increase awareness, and so on. As with most new technologies, there will be insidious applications too: government agencies will no doubt experiment with chemicals intended to make people more "cooperative," thereby serving the needs of these agencies in their intelligence and counterintelligence work.

BIOLOGY

Biology is likely to provide the most exciting and dramatic breakthroughs in science in the next two decades, paralleling the growth of understanding of physics in the first third of this century. Some of this knowledge will be applied to biological technology.

Understanding biological processes, especially sensory discrimination and organism control, through the application to biological processes of cybernetic and information theory and microinstrumental and computer techniques, is already producing new ideas applicable to the design of machines. These developments will, in turn, accelerate the growth of understanding of the processes by which men think, discriminate, seek goals, and generally select from and guide themselves through the world of things and symbols. (5) (For example, radically new computer circuits that discriminate among data have been based on the discovery of a heretofore unknown nerve mechanism by which frogs see only moving objects.)

Telemetering and computer techniques for monitoring, diagnosing, and treating biological malfunctions are already in use; these will be greatly refined and extended. Many people will live with sensors permanently embedded in their bodies, transmitting information through them to the outside. Much more than now, doctors will depend on information obtained through complex physical measurements of body processes directly transmitted to computers for analysis. Some physiological measures taken by the sensors may be read to the doctor by the patient, even as people now read thermometers.

Increased understanding of biological growth and organization will produce important improvements in the prevention and control of disease. Organ transplants may be feasible in some cases. If so, organ banks, similar to blood, bone, and cornea banks, are likely.

Oral contraceptives for both sexes will become cheap, effective, and physiologically safe. Contraceptives which are physiologically implanted in the body and which are effective over long periods are likely developments. A special incentive to their development is their potential value in societies where it is difficult to establish habits of oral dosage-taking.

It is plausible that in the next twenty years a baby's sex may be predetermined or, at least, the probability increased that a baby will be of the chosen sex.

Non-habit-forming, generally nontoxic, hallucination-producing (or "experience-widening") chemicals, already available in limited amounts and variety, may be produced cheaply in quantity.

Synthetic photosynthesis is a likely development. Whether it will be used to manufacture human nourishment—except on an emergency, stand-by basis—is not at all clear.

Toward the end of the next twenty years, some systematic attempts will be under way to improve crops and livestock by deliberately altering the genetic "code" carried by the chemical agents of heredity.

COMMUNICATIONS

Insofar as use by the public is concerned, trends in communications appear to be: more telephone lines, television and radio channels, and facsimile circuitry.

More and more, the world will become one communications net of high speed data transmitters, cybernated libraries, and data displays. Communication satellites belonging to several nations will play a major role, especially as refinements in related satellite technologies permit more power in lighter payloads (which only need relatively small rockets to put them into orbit).

It is likely that, during the next ten years at least, world-wide satellite communications will favor profitable telephone circuits rather than wide-scale educational and cultural TV and more conventional entertainment. No amount of technological development will surmount time differences between Europe, Asia, and North America. Except for critical events which would make TV watching worth while at odd hours, it probably will be more economical to tape programs and fly them to other nations than to use economically valuable satellite circuits to transmit taped TV programs. However, transmissions between North and South America and between Europe and Africa do fall in the same time zones. Therefore, there may be more north-south than east-west live intercultural and educational television by satellite. The opportunities for augmenting educational facilities in the underdeveloped areas seem especially great, at least in principle.

As the technologies of microminiaturized transmitters and receivers, biomedical telemetering, and computerized data processing evolve, they may be increasingly applied clandestinely to obtain information about governments and people if the anxieties and pressures produced by internal and external threats and frustrations become great enough to encourage this. The already extensive use of the tapped telephone, the hidden recorder, the reconnaissance satellite, are precursors of a special communications technology feasible in the next two decades. (6) Of course, "counterdevices" will also be invented and applied. Indeed, the wavering battle between "offensive" and "defensive" devices will simply compound efforts to obtain information by these means —including information about the equipment, personnel, and strategies used.

WEAPONS

With or without arms-control arrangements, the next two decades will see major developments in weapons and weapons-related technology. Without arms control it is very likely that a number of governments will have nuclear weapons—developed by themselves, bought with the aid of scientific and engineering mercenaries, or obtained from other nations. It is by no means impossible that some criminal organizations will own primitive nuclear weapons.

Missiles and other strategic vehicles for delivery will become ever more sophisticated, as will antistrategic delivery vehicles technology. The pros and cons of strategies and counterstrategies and counter-counterstrategies based on these weapons will become more complex and more based on computer analysis. Although in some aspects these strategies will be responsive to improved knowledge in behavioral science, they will often be profoundly detached from social reality, chiefly because there will still be no good basis for predicting societies' reactions to large-scale nuclear disaster.

Substantial levels of arms control or disarmament will take years to establish. During this period, there should be enormous improvements in supersensitive sensors of all types, capable of detecting biological, chemical, and electromagnetic traces whose presence or absence in specific environments will be important for the conduct of overt and clandestine warfare and for the verification of arms-control arrangements.

It is also very likely that there will be extensive developments in chemical and biological agents for clandestine and counterinsurgency warfare, for intelligence and counterintelligence, and perhaps as agents of pacification used by an international police force. These agents are likely to be nonlethal for most people exposed to them. They will be physically and emotionally disabling or debilitating. (Among other uses, they would be effective against underdeveloped nations especially dependent on the availability of manpower for specific tasks at specific times, such as crop planting and harvesting.) That they will also alter the morals of those who use them is hardly speculation.

TRANSPORTATION

There will be more cars. In the countries that can afford them, and particularly in the U.S. and Western Europe, automobiles will continue to be the most attractive form of private conveyance and, in spite of growing congestion, will be the most typical way of getting around in most metropolitan areas. However, it is also very likely that noncommercial vehicles will be banned in midtown areas in the most traffic-jammed cities.

More mass transportation will be used, but only gradually. The political, social, and economic problems involved in installing and operating mass rapid-transit systems will for some years continue to delay such programs, at least while transport is second to more traditional city priorities. The subway and the bus will be the most frequent forms of mass transport.

Toward the end of the next ten years there probably will be a few regularly operating, interurban 200-mile-an-hour "trains," some of which will ride a fraction of an inch off their tracks or monorail on cushions of air. The politics and economics of buying rights of way, strengthening and redesigning roadbeds, and arranging interstate participation are likely to prevent large-scale development by the 1980's. However, because of the problems of controlling increasingly dense air traffic, pressures will intensify to develop such high-speed, safe, and frequent interurban traffic. Enough air disasters or, less compellingly, enough exasperation may well result in more rapid development of high-speed "railroads." Vertical-takeoff aircraft probably will supplement interurban transportation facilities eventually. They may substantially contribute to intramegalopolis transport in the 1970's, but traffic control problems and costs will discourage their use as mass transport.

Aircraft flying at two or three times the speed of sound on transoceanic runs may be a commercial reality by the early 1970's. Unless the destructive sound wave which accompanies them is weakened (and there is no efficient way to do this now), they probably will not be used for cross-country flights.

An important transportation development already beginning to be used commercially, especially in Europe (and likely to be used widely in the future), is cheap, high-speed water transportation via hydrofoil craft. (The hydrofoil craft skims along the water's surface with only skids sliding through the water, in contrast to conventional ships whose hulls drag through the water.) There appear to be no serious engineering difficulties barring the construction of river-going and ocean-going passenger ships moving at 40-60 knots.

The technology of space travel will involve very few people as passengers, but very many indirectly. By about 1970, after enormous intellectual and material investments, the United States or the USSR, or both, will have landed men on the moon. Some men will be spending days to months in satellite orbits. By the early 1980's it is just possible that a very, very few men will have reached Mars—alive. A few more will be living for months at a time on the moon in small outposts devoted to scientific research.

RESIDENTIAL TECHNOLOGY

A vast variety of radical construction methods and fabrication materials which could revolutionize the building industry, especially the construction of private dwellings, already exists. The application of this technology in the next two decades depends on whether or not archaic and conflicting building codes and Federal construction standards are revised, and on whether or not power can be wrested from selfish and short-sighted construction unions and construction and supply businesses who abet the present restrictions on choice of materials and construction methods. (7) If these blocs are broken and codes are standardized and updated, the mass production of prefabricated components (such as one-piece bathrooms and walls complete with built-in plumbing and electrical wiring) will be economically feasible. Then the quality per dollar of construction costs should improve greatly. These pressures may become sufficiently great as the costs of housing and community services increase; as the number of dwellings needed for the new population makes old methods and materials too inefficient; and if building more new towns and cities becomes an attractive public or private investment. Federal Government and private builders, building beyond the jurisdiction of local codes, and the influence of local construction firms, may encourage major changes in construction technology, especially if workers are not displaced and wages lowered. Government research and development subsidies to defense industries looking for new markets to invade, in order to compensate for reductions in military research and development, could substantially increase the pressures to use new construction technologies. But the changeover probably will not be rapid, given interlocking, entrenched interests and conventional operating styles.

On the other hand, over the next two decades the opportunities for cybernation in the home will increase. The technological potential exists and the possibilities are good for increasing the amount of discretionary spending on the home (rather than, say, on the car). More automatic servicing of the home—packaged services for food, cleaning, and so on—is very likely, too. The telephone will be used much more as a command and control device, permitting remote initiation and monitoring of a variety of household tasks.

POWER

If controlled nuclear fusion were to become practicable over the next twenty years it would have profound effects for the world. If it operated as scientists now believe it would, it could provide cheap power in practically unlimited amounts for any geographic area needing it, and would have none of the dangers and difficulties involved in the radioactive by-products of fission-type reactors. At present there is considerable pessimism about harnessing such energy in the foreseeable future; no known approach to the problem seems truly promising. It is mentioned here because so much research is under way on this topic; because if a breakthrough should occur it might well be applied fairly quickly; and because if fusion power were to be easily and cheaply available, much of this book would need major revisions in the light of the unprecedented consequences of plentiful, cheap power for all peoples.

WEATHER

The combined use of weather satellites, high-speed data processing, and extended ground facilities will make possible local, short-range weather *forecasts* in many parts of the world. It is plausible that reliable seasonal weather forecasts will be available on a world-wide basis sometime during the next twenty years. But it is unlikely that weather *control* will also be possible or practiced (beyond, perhaps, local rain-making and fog dispersal). The knowledge needed to do so will be at least of the kind needed to make long-range forecasts. Moreover, if weather can be changed at all by known human powers, no one can now predict that its geographic scope or consequences, once changed, could be controlled.

WATER

The technology of water purifying and repurifying will expand greatly. Conversion of seawater to fresh water, already under way, will be necessary to supplement water supplies in many parts of the world, including the United States, especially in the West and Southwest. Purifying and recycling used fresh water will also become a major technology. However, extensive application will come only after prolonged political in-fighting. The costs of equipment and facilities and operations for contaminant removal will add to costs for communities and private enterprise. Often, too, it will be a long and difficult task to determine the effects of contaminants on humans and wild life. (A not unlikely thalidomide-type disaster would probably provide the political leverage to accelerate the application of this technology.)

OCEANOGRAPHY

Investments in oceanographic technology, especially by the government, are likely to increase very substantially over the next twenty years. These investments will be aimed at mining and farming the oceans and possibly at developing undersea colonies for this work and for research. Developing equipment for undersea living would involve allocations of resources analogous to those for space activities, and it is conceivable that various governments will come to see such investments as in their domestic, economic, and international interests.

Here, too, multinational research and engineering efforts are likely to increase.

RECREATION

Recreational technology will offer enormous opportunities for engineering imagination and entrepreneurship. If our economy remains reasonably prosperous, so that people with shorter work weeks have incomes to spend on leisure, the production of leisure-time equipment and facilities doubtless will expand very greatly. Emphasis on leisure as the time for self-expression and, sometimes, for exhilarating risk-taking—both of which will become less and less a part of working experience for more and more people—should stimulate new opportunities for technology. For example, novel transport devices may offer especially attractive means for getting to recreation areas and may provide new recreational activities themselves. The fast-growing sport of skin-diving might be complemented by sports using craft that skim over water and land, floating on a cushion of air; synthetic snow, permitting year-round skiing, might be developed; and so on.

References

1. Price, Derek J. De Solla, "Diseases of Science," in *Science Since Babylon*. New Haven: Yale University Press, 1961.

2. Greenberg, D. S., "Civilian Technology: Concern Over Pace of Growth Inspires Program for Research and Development Effort," *Science,* Vol. 139, No. 3555, Washington, D.C. February 15, 1963, p. 576.

3. Bright, James R., "Are We Falling Behind in Mechanization?" *Harvard Business Review,* Vol. 40, No. 6, Cambridge, Mass., November-December 1960, pp. 93–106.

4. Pines, Maya, "How Three-Year-Olds Teach Themselves to Read—and Love It," *Harper's.* Vol. 226, No. 1356, New York, May 1963, pp. 58–64.

5. David, Heather M., "Bionics: Symposium Points to More AF Emphasis on Hardware," *Missiles and Rockets,* Vol. 12, No. 13, Washington, D.C., April 1, 1963, pp. 34–35.

6. Packard, Vance, *The Naked Society.* New York: David McKay Co., 1964. Brenton, Myron, *The Privacy Invaders.* New York: Coward-McCann, 1964.

7. Watkins, A. M., "A Good House Nowadays Is Hard to Find," *Harper's,* Vol. 220, No. 1317, New York, February 1960, pp. 37-43.

Supplementary References

Aron, Raymond, George Kennan, Robert Oppenheimer, *et al., World Technology and Human Destiny.* Ann Arbor: University of Michigan Press, 1963.

Engineering Research Committee, *The Nation's Engineering Research Needs 1965–1985,* Summary Report, Engineers Joint Council, Inc. New York, May 25, 1962.

Kilian, James, Jr., "The Crisis in Research," *Atlantic Monthly*, Vol. 211, No. 3, Boston, March 1963, pp. 69–72.

Michael, Donald N., *Cybernation: The Silent Conquest*. Santa Barbara, Calif.: Center for the Study of Democratic Institutions, 1962.

Piel, Gerard, *Science in the Cause of Man*. New York: Alfred A. Knopf, 1961.

3

RATIONALIZATION: THE GENERALIZED APPLICATION OF ORGANIZED EFFICIENCY

IT IS inevitable that much greater effort will be put into applying the methods of science and engineering to set all sorts of goals and to organize men, work methods, and administration so that those goals can be attained by the most efficient means. This highly logical approach to applying the most efficient means for determining and realizing ends is usually referred to as "rationalization." (It is not to be confused with the psychological processes described by the same word, though the appeal to logic as an excuse for efficiency has been and doubtless will again be a form of rationalization in the psychological sense.) It should be clearly understood that rationalization is only a technique—albeit, a particularly powerful one. Of itself this technique has no necessary connection with wisdom. It can be applied to outrageous, idiotic, satanic, wonderful, wise, or angelic goals. Value preferences are always implicit in its application, whatever the ostensibly logical or necessary goals. And values themselves are nonlogical and not necessarily consistent in a person or in an organization. Two fundamental consequences arise in this context. The assiduous application of rationalization need not lead to a world of enlightened interest and sweet reason. In particular, it need not lead to the reorganization of competing organizations into a harmonious whole which pursues whatever task the members previously pursued separately. Each rationalized agency may more intensively and efficiently pursue its own gains, still driven, by whatever myths, whims, or traditions define the goals of the organization. In the second place, rationalization can and has tricked many into thinking they were being reasonable, if not wise. It has also helped wise and reasonable people in the pursuit of their goals. The point here is that rationalization will be used more than ever, foolishly or sensibly.   *organized effort*

The widening availability of computers, growing formal understanding of the behavior of men as individuals and in groups, the emphasis on science and logic as well as growing needs for efficient use of large numbers of people and material will result in greater emphasis on systematic organization and operation. A growing population with growing requirements to assure it adequate distribution and consumption of materials, information, and symbols; growing problems in the managing of cities and megalopoli; the tendency to push vocational screening and training as far as possible toward the beginning of school; the inadequacy of the family as the controlling and guiding agency for adolescents and children—all these and many other factors will put great pressure on institutions to rationalize their operations.

Mass education, large research and development laboratories, mass transportation, mass religion, mass recreation facilities, big business, even small businesses (which will rent centralized computer services for rationalizing their operations) will be increasingly operated in ways intended to maximize command, control, predictability, and stability. Clearly, this trend and the conflicts between it and less organized approaches to life will greatly influence the experiences, opportunities, and viewpoints of youth and the adults guiding them.

The expected scope of economic and social welfare demands of this society, compared to the projected numbers of highly qualified professionals which the educational system will be able to turn out, makes it clear that there will be desperate shortages of top-flight managers, engineers, and many other professionals. As a result, there will be strong pressures to use those who are available far more efficiently than they are now used. Of course this increased efficiency won't come about to the degree truly required, because we won't know how to achieve it; because some who could be used more efficiently in other jobs in other places won't want to make the change; and often because present employers, in and out of government, will fight giving up their skilled people. Nevertheless, within organizations and among them, there will be developments aimed at rationalizing the use of scarce manpower, by selecting more carefully those things to which they apply their skills and by more carefully organizing their efforts. Thus, shortages of skilled, high-level manpower will lead to attempts at more careful and deliberate selection of programs and allocations of effort—a major factor in the rationalization of any activity, big or small.

POSITIVE AND NEGATIVE CONSEQUENCES

Better understanding of those factors which influence human behavior and better computer-based methods for obtaining information will provide planners and decision-makers with knowledge about the state of society in its various parts rapidly enough to allow more appropriate and precise actions. Simulation of alternative social responses to different decisions will provide them with improved bases for selecting strategies of social control. Rationalization of public welfare and commercial activities, facilitated by detailed information about the private citizen, is already under way. (1) It remains to be seen whether this control will be used to encourage greater individual freedom and spontaneity outside the areas of rationalization and greater focused activity within, or whether the trend will be toward more over-all restriction. Both attractive and unattractive consequences will be evident.

It is especially important to point out that the meaning of "rationalization" will be frequently misunderstood. Both opponents and proponents of more rationalization will interpret it, more often than not, to mean the assiduous application of logic at the expense of attention to and operation of such extra-logical factors as personal preferences and needs. Too narrow an interpretation of rationalized methods will lead to fiascos when these methods ignore the extra-rational needs of society and of those working in an "efficient" environment. Gradually, the more alert rationalizing organizations will discover that rationalization works better when applied in a broad sense, i.e., so it includes the extrarational. At first, however, fad and operational pressures will strongly equate rationalization with "cold" logic. (In discovering the proper balance, the behavioral sciences will play a crucial role.)

One serious mistake will doubtless occur often as organizations try to rationalize their activities and programs: they will so organize that innovation and initiative are throttled by commitment to computer-derived or computer-implemented programs of action, and by the costs in prestige, time, and money involved in changing a long-range computer program in the light of new ideas. This situation already exists in government and industry; many programs could probably be done better if it were possible to overcome the economic and psychological commitment to the computer-based operations already under way.

At its worst, increasing rationalization would abet and encourage totalitarianism. For example, if many nations own nuclear and other "unconventional" weapons, pressure may be increased to maintain and expand national military security. This factor of security, plus ideological and economic competition from other nations, plus the frustrations and difficulties the United States will face internally, may strongly encourage the growth of a "garrison state." (2) An extensive espionage or "snooping" technology focused on detecting individual deviations from accepted standards of efficiency and purpose would certainly help establish and maintain such a state.

If we avoid the garrison state, we can expect the persistence of substantial, if lessening, "chaos" in the midst of "order." Even today, in what are taken to be well-rationalized organizations (e.g., the Department of Defense or the planning departments of some corporations), values and behaviors that are not subservient to the "logical" needs of the system persist. And, too, enlargement of the scope of rationalized activities will not advance proportionately in all sectors of the society. There will be forces resisting as well as forces embracing long-range coordinated and controlled social planning.

The very fact that society will be so big, so complex, and tending to be more rationalized also means it will be able to tolerate groups living at different paces and styles, if they show no deliberate intent to alter significantly the drive or direction of the prevailing social processes. (They may do so inadvertently, of course.) Isolated and insulated from major and majority preoccupations of the society, and thereby offering no threat to the *status quo,* these enclaves will provide opportunities for more whimsical, personally paced styles of life.

There will be, then, many relatively small and scattered experiments in the conduct of education and in the seeking of satisfying private experiences. Only a small fraction of the population will be involved—those most dissatisfied with the rationalized (narrowly defined) society who, at the same time, have the sensitivity, imagination, and motivation to seek modes of expression at variance with the general direction of the society, but who have no need for quick demonstrations to themselves that they are remaking society. Indeed, the fact that these experiments will repudiate, or at least modify, the rationalized life will be used by spokesmen for the "establishment" as argument that the society is still

highly heterogeneous and responsive to the idiosyn-
cratic needs of the individual and is only rationalized to
the extent desired or necessary.

The trend will, nevertheless, be strongly in the direction of rationalization. For one thing, such an approach
will appeal to—or, at least, will not often be resisted by
—the products of an education that stresses science or,
more particularly, engineering, wherein manipulation
of things and control of the environment are stressed.
For another, there is no reason to believe this society
will become clearer and more united in its definitions of
ultimate goals. On the contrary, among many people
actively concerned with these matters the articulation
between policies and deeply felt and thought-through
goals probably will decrease as the complexities of living increase. (Often enough, the process of rationalizing a given activity will demonstrate how complex it
really is!) As a result, the traditionally strong tendency
in the United States to concentrate on programs rather
than on their goals may well increase in many quarters.
And programs are precisely what can be well imple-
mented through the rationalizing of the techniques discussed. Their success will tend to draw attention away
from questions about the fundamental "whys" of the
programs.

Greater understanding and control of the logical factors affecting a program will offer some people the opportunity for more emphasis on the extra-logical, moral,
and ethical consequences of a program. In some quarters, then, there will be increasing attention to the relationship between programs and goals; "values" and
"purposes" will, for some decision-makers, become
much more important than they are now. How effectively
they synthesize programs and goals, within their organi-

zation and in relation to other organizations, and
whether the power structures they serve will permit
these preoccupations, remains to be seen. Certainly,
their task will be difficult, but just as certainly, there
will be a crucial need for these rare philosopher-kings.

There will be attractions in the rationalized life, especially as the individual's opinion of his competence to
deal personally with the huge and complex world decreases, and specialized training increases his sense of
competence to deal effectively with his own task within
an organizational framework. Moreover, much of the
experience of a large portion of the population will be
within such a framework, and to live otherwise will be
uncomfortable for many, even as it is today. But there
are also dissatisfactions inherent in such a system, especially when rationalization emphasizes the "logical"
aspects of efficiency. The excitement of the unexpected,
the invigorating state of mind produced by shifts in
pleasure, pain, tranquility, and anxiety are largely miss-
ing. Underlying the rewards of being a cog in the wheel
can be a sense of boredom and thinness of self.

Under these circumstances, novelty and sensation
will be especially sought after—even if the novelty is
"packaging" only and the sensation is for the most part
vicarious or standardized or rapidly becomes standardized through the style-setting mass media. These media,
in turn, will continue to appeal partially through their
ability to inform the uninitiated of novelties they can
possess—thereby routinizing them. Internal pressures
to seek novelty and sensation as a release from the
expectedness of rationalized activities will be encouraged by external commercial enticements. This tendency
will increase as industry seeks new ways to use its growing productive capacities. These needs and the re-

sponses to them will further encourage an economy heavily oriented toward private consumption.

RATIONALIZATION OF CRIME

Like other large organizations, "big crime" will continue its present trend toward greater rationalization. Racketeering, usury, gambling, and prostitution will not disappear, but if people find they do not have to turn for their gratifications to sources of supply outside the approved (or at least tolerated) social institutions, the opportunities for burgeoning criminal activities based on supplying tabooed experiences will decrease. Sooner or later, for example, narcotics will lose their profit when addiction is treated as a disease rather than a crime and needed amounts are medically available. Gambling is likely to be legalized gradually in more and more places, and prostitution will become less lucrative as the value of chastity declines.

Big crime will become harder to distinguish from more acceptable, if shady, social, political, and financial practices. This will be especially true as opportunities increase for making especially good profits in more legitimate investments (from the nontaxed money acquired earlier in criminal activities) and as rationalization of these activities puts more operating constraints on personnel and entrepreneurship.

ROLE OF GOVERNMENT

The inexorable expansion of the Federal Government as the dominant device for social control will be a major factor in the increasing rationalization of society. More and more, major social problems and opportunities will have to be met on a national scale if they are to be met adequately. Long lead-time planning and phased implementation of the plans will be vitally important in order to keep society from jamming up here and running down there as our population grows and as everything becomes more interrelated, complex, and demanding of scarce time and resources. Such planning will require detailed knowledge about local parts of the socioeconomic system and the power to effect those local parts in order to affect the national system, and vice versa.

Detailed, nation-wide information about government and business intentions and potentials (to the extent they can be elicited from business), combined with advanced systems analysis methods, will increasingly be applied to the planning and implementation of long-range national programs—whether they be for the conservation of water resources or human resources, the development of space programs or medical programs, the subsidy of education or supersonic air transport, the advancement of the purposes of private industry or those of government.

Many methods of rationalization (in both the broad and narrow senses) have been developed and applied in some corporations. This trend will certainly continue, driven by big business' needs to deal with its own growth and by small enterprises' (what remains of them) attempts to survive among markets and technology increasingly dominated by big enterprise. Additional multinational interlocking among private enterprises will provide further stimulus. The growing interdependence of big enterprise and the Federal Government, and the continuing application of rationalizing methods to this relationship to improve its efficiency, will further blur distinctions between the two. This process has been most evident in the defense industry–government nexus; it is now evident, too, in such essentially civilian agencies as the National Aeronautics and Space Administration.

However, this blurring of functions and operations will grow more slowly than the need for certain national actions. For example, many major problems and opportunities for national and human development will require more deliberate coordination than will be volunteered by free enterprise at any given time. These the government will have to develop and direct, because only the Federal Government will have resources and responsibilities to meet these requirements. It will be under increasing pressure to assign priorities to and stimulate such programs as urban renewal and new town construction through the use of legal, tax, subsidy, and regulating procedures. To carry out such projects on the grand scale required will necessitate assiduous application of rationalization techniques. (3)

In particular, government will play the major role in coping with the problems of disemployment, unemployment, and lower wages, whatever the sources. The government will collect detailed data to assess the situation, plan retraining and relocation programs, and determine how the contingent costs are to be shared. As other sections of this book suggest, the chances are that unemployment and disemployment will become sufficiently serious in the next ten years to require public works programs (such as improving national park facilities and cleaning up and revitalizing slum areas), especially for unskilled young people.

In the fairly likely event of a significant shift to a disarmed economy, the Federal Government will have to coordinate the transition and choose public investment activities needed to stimulate the economy and to meet the new national interests. It will also have the responsibility of meeting the human problems of relocation, retraining, and financial need during the adjustment period.

The role of government as the chief "social control" agency in the society will not enlarge suddenly, evenly, or ubiquitously. Those elected to government will for many years be chiefly the products of our past, and they will reflect the perspectives of a population that will still be chiefly a product of the past. Thus, further rationalizing of government activities will be unattractive to many politicians and their constituents, and rationalizing trends will be slowed by their objections and tactics. And, of course, many powerful bureaucrats will have much to gain by delaying further rationalization in the offices and agencies in which their status and operating styles are deeply invested.

The problems and opportunities foreseen in this book have so far been sensed, vaguely and selectively, by only a small fraction of the population. Various public groups and various parts of the Federal and local governments will differ as to when and in what ways government involvement must be enlarged and rationalized (as frequent legislative–executive differences amply demonstrate). Moreover, many of the changes to come will simply be reinforcements of trends already under way. It will take time for the general public and for the government to appreciate that changes in degree and in meaning, in the light of other trends, will be profound. This appreciation will rest, in large part, on the effective application of more rationalized methods to the process of government itself, and on the nature of other institutions' responses to government involvement.

References

1. Seib, Charles B., "The Martinsburg Monster," *Harper's*, April 1962, pp. 33–36.

2. Lasswell, Harold D., "The Garrison-State Hypothesis Today," in Samuel P. Huntington, ed., *Changing Patterns of Military Politics*. New York: The Free Press of Glencoe, Inc., 1962, pp. 51–70.

3. Chase, Edward T., "Politics and Technology," *The Yale Review*, Vol. LII, No. 3, March 1963.

Supplementary References

Mayo, Louis H., "The New Technology and Multi-National Cooperation," *Minnesota Law Review*, Vol. 46, No. 5, April 1962, pp. 869–912.

Philipson, Morris, ed., *Automation: Implications for the Future*. New York: Vintage Books, 1962.

CHAPTER

4

URBAN TRENDS

IN THE next twenty years the United States will become steadily more megalopolized. By 1980, about 75 per cent of our people will be living within the expanding metropolitan areas growing from core cities and in newly constructed cities and towns interspersed around the present ones. From this geographical spreading and fusing, and from the concomitant population growth and organizational complexity, will grow acute ecological and social problems that cannot be solved within the framework of conventional political units. Transportation, air and water pollution, water and land use, labor and leisure utilization, statistics, crime control, urban renewal and redevelopment—all are examples of problems beginning to be or already incapable of adequate solution within the constraints of arbitrary political boundaries of city and state. As these problems become crises, extra-political institutions organized to deal with them will become far more prevalent.

There will be, to be sure, more political experiments attempting to transcend conventional state and local governing units. But the shift to regional or subregional governments will be slow, for the political and economic resistance of entrenched interests is enormous. (1) The radical new arrangements needed would expel many a bureaucrat and political appointee, and they know it. Then, too, many businesses live off contracts from the present governments, contracts fattened by or dependent upon the inefficiency or inadequacy of state and local governments. And they know it. The recent trend toward congressional reapportionment, favoring the city, will not be significant for many years. At the least, the customary battle between rural and urban areas may simply be replaced by new struggles between suburb and central city.

Encouragement for change will come in the forms of Federal Government funds and technical advice for needed programs, contingent on more efficient governing machinery. Urban planner Melvin Webber has suggested that some larger governing units may develop when white political machines try to retain power, in the face of Negro dominance in central cities, by extending city boundaries to include surrounding white suburbs. But for the most part, the needs of regions and subregions will be ameliorated through increasing use of special-purpose agencies which span political boundaries; the New York Port Authority, the Chicago Transit Authority, the Milwaukee Metropolitan Sewerage Division are examples of what is to come.

Emphasis on "social planning" for new and old cities, areas, and regions, corresponding to the emphasis in recent years on physical planning, can also be expected. (2) Growing interest in delinquency control, community mental health, and related activities will encourage more experiments in which physical planning is subordinate to social planning—but not without intense arguments and in-fighting among the professions and politicians involved. However, as social planning begins to demonstrate its capacity to smooth transitions and operations it will become more used and useful. These various circumstances will lead to growing opportunities for professional and technical personnel in regional and subregional institutions and on staffs of city-building and community-development organizations.

Thus, there will be more rationalization of activities for planning, guiding, and controlling the development and operation of region-wide activities and of new cities. For these reasons there will also be fewer job opportunities for the untrained and unskilled in traditional political-appointee institutions, as they find it increasingly necessary to mesh their activities with various "Authorities."

Even the relatively well-educated citizen may find metropolitan and regional problems too technical and complex to follow closely, except when they become scandalous or critical. Apathy will be a typical response, but there will also be more informed participation by some citizens in strictly local problems, for example, in schools, libraries, and police protection. Involvement in local issues may compensate some citizens for their sense of impotence in influencing affairs at the national, metropolitan, or regional level. It is not at all clear that local interest in local issues will be sufficiently enlightened or inclusive to encourage attention to problems in less intellectually and economically endowed neighborhoods. But if domestic "peace corps" activities (the poverty program's Volunteers for America) are not crushed in local political vises, they may set the style for all kinds of volunteer "consulting" in which the "haves" gain a sense of potency from helping the "have nots" with their local problems (much as an occasional white has helped some American Indians to protect their rights).

Local civic involvement may also be accelerated by a tendency for big business to encourage its executive personnel to be active in local civic projects. The pressure to do so may increase as business faces more problems in community relations as a result of its introduction of new technologies that produce changes in the shop and the front office. (Using for this purpose middle-level managers, who would otherwise be displaced by cybernation, might save top management the discomfort of firing these men and also provide some public relations bonus.)

Of course, very large parts of the population will be unmoved by these governmental and operational changes, even as they are unmoved by the issues presently facing cities and suburbs.

Of the many problems associated with the growth of the megalopolis, two at least are unavoidably bound to become critical during the period under discussion.

In many urban regions a fresh-water shortage will be sufficiently serious to require great investments in purifying and recycling systems, water purification, and usage control. Efficient use of scarce or more expensive water supplies will make mandatory long-range planning and governmental involvement in all kinds of water-using activities. The cost of water will increase, and with the increase may well come inhibitions on the private use of it (in curious contrast to a life style stressing high consumption of almost all other commodities).

The second problem that will have to be faced squarely during this period is application of wide-ranging solutions to the social and economic ghettoizing of

some lower-class groups, especially Negroes. In spite of
Federal actions, growing local white support for change,
and some acceptance of Negroes in previously all-white
neighborhoods, white suburbs and middle-class residential areas are not even beginning to absorb Negroes at a
rate comparable to the rate of growth of central-city,
high-density Negro residential areas. For one thing,
most Negroes cannot afford more expensive housing.
The enormous problems involved in providing slum children with adequate education, and adolescents and
adults with adequate job training, means that both
young and older Negroes will bear disproportionately
the economic and psychological consequences of unemployment and disemployment of the unskilled, at least
over the next decade. (3) Poor education and poor income and the associated style of life, with its concomitants of delinquency and violence, will encourage many
white entrepreneurs and politicians to fight for the pres-
ervation of present housing patterns. Indeed, major extensions of urban renewal and redevelopment will be in-
definitely delayed—with all the adverse consequences
for urban areas resulting from slums and ghettos—
until this problem is resolved.

This situation is bound to become more socially complicated and emotionally intense as the growing Negro
proportion of city populations results in more Negroes'
being elected to important posts, and, in some cases, in
their domination of the government. With increased political power will come opportunities for Negro politicians to channel funds into Negro education and retraining. They will also have more opportunity to force
private organizations, dependent for contracts on city
regulations, codes, and funds, to open their doors to
Negro participation. Whether the transition will be pre-

dominantly conservative and tranquil or demagogic and violent remains to be seen. But the growing strength of Negro action groups guarantees that Negro needs will crucially affect all urban developments in the next years. Part of the range of likely responses can be inferred from the history of the political behavior of once-deprived groups such as the Irish, Italians, and Jews. In part, the responses will depend on the values of the whites who do not leave the city for the suburbs and of those who return from the suburbs (as their children grow into adults) to live in select white urban areas. It will also depend on the extent of and conditions for Federal aid for urban needs.

It also remains to be seen what effects Negro-dominated city governments will have on the growth and direction of interstate and regional Authorities and of intercity cooperation.

References

1. Banfield, Edward C., and Morton Grodzins, *Government and Housing in Metropolitan Areas.* New York: McGraw-Hill Book Co., Inc., 1958, Chapters 1, 10.

2. Duhl, Leonard T., ed., *The Urban Condition.* New York: Basic Books, Inc., 1963.

3. Grier, Eunice S. "Factors Hindering Integration in Urban Areas," *Journal of Intergroup Relations,* Vol. 2, No. 4, 1961, pp. 293–301.

Supplementary References

Editors of *Fortune, The Exploding Metropolis.* New York: Doubleday & Company, Inc., 1958.

Finley, William E., *The Comprehensive Plan as an Instrument of Social Planning Policy.* Washington, D.C.: Washington Center for Metropolitan Studies, April 1962.

"The Future Metropolis," *Daedalus,* Gerald Holton, ed.,

American Academy of Arts and Sciences, Vol. 90, No. 1, Boston, Winter, 1961.

Hacker, Andrew, *Congressional Districting: The Issue of Equal Representation.* Washington, D.C.: The Brookings Institution, June 1963, p. 115.

Jacobs, Jane, *Death and Life of Great American Cities.* New York: Random House, 1961.

CHAPTER

5

UNDERDEVELOPED
NATIONS

DEVELOPMENTS in Asia, Africa, and Latin America
over the next two decades will be significant for youth in
three ways. First, there will be work possibilities for those
with the appropriate training, personalities, and aspirations. Second, the activities of these nations will influence the values and beliefs of some Americans about
the nature of man, governments, human rights, and
progress—and whether American ways of doing and believing are the "natural" ways of societies. In the third
place, these nations will increasingly influence the pursuit of our national purposes. Successful expression of
our political and material power will increasingly depend on our willingness to consider the national interests
of countries outside the "big power" complex. In particular, it will become even clearer that the UN is not our
exclusive instrument of power and that noncommunist
nations do not always agree with our definition of "right"
or act in the UN in concert with our interests.

Unless there are overwhelming changes in the over-all approach of the developed nations toward the under-developed—which seems unlikely in the next decade at least—the next twenty years for the underdeveloped nations will continue to be difficult, fraught with crucial shortages of capital, teachers, skilled labor and professional personnel, and the attitudes and values needed to encourage the accumulation of these. According to Robert L. Heilbroner (who expresses the private concerns of other experts):

The probabilities are great that we shall have to stand more or less impotently by while the dynamics of development work their troubled way, "surrounding" us in Asia, Africa, and South America with governments whose policies and programs point in a general direction counter to that which we ourselves desire. (1)

There will continue to be excess population, chauvinism, unstable governments, extremist political activities, authoritarian leaders, and critical resources wasted in efforts to produce at least the symbolic accouterments of developed nations. Population growth, coupled with very limited resources of food and shelter, practically guarantees recurring major famines and tragic losses from other natural disasters during the next two decades. (Cheap and practical contraceptive methods may very well be available to these populations, but the time needed to overcome ignorance and social and religious inhibitions will delay for many years any significant decrease in population growth.) Although standards of living probably will improve, on the average the improvement will be slight indeed. Most important, the gap between the have and have-not nations will continue to increase.

Many leaders of the underdeveloped nations hold emotionally inflated aspirations and expectations; they have yet to realize that both external and internal limitations virtually insure a very slow rate of development for their nations over the next two decades. Sooner or later, realism will begin to erode the hopes of these leaders and the slow growth will be evident to their followers as well. The consequences are bound to be great, very probably adverse, resulting frequently in social depression and despair or, more likely, in violence and demagoguery. The impact on the developed nations will probably be considerable, for neither of these responses is likely to inspire compassionate support. Large moral issues portend, for the underdeveloped peoples are in good part non-Christian and colored. They will make demands of and be judged by developed white nations, faced with their own exasperations and frustrations—which are always easier to blame and to take out on others.

There will be, in principle, expanding opportunities for Americans of all ages who are appropriately trained and motivated and who can get along well in other cultures, to contribute to the development of these nations through public and private activities (exemplified by the Peace Corps). Whether these opportunities exist in fact will depend on the attitudes of these nations toward public or private United States assistance and this, of course, will depend on the philosophies of their governments and on how the United States conducts its international relations.

Whatever our level of support for the underdeveloped nations, it will increasingly have to emphasize long-range commitments based on the application of complex economic, political, social, and technological considerations. This does not mean that the decisions will necessarily be "inhuman." Indeed, to the extent that social engineering is applied, the chances are good that what is done will be more meaningful and more satisfying for the underdeveloped nations involved. But it may well be that, with our growing awareness that things in these countries are not too likely to go our way, decisions will frequently be based on pragmatic considerations rather than on values about the proper moral conduct of men and nations. Rationalization of these government plans and programs will result in more dependence on highly professional competencies, and thus will make it more difficult for the public and its elected representatives, who lack such competencies, to judge meaningfully the validity of the foreign aid policies proposed. Such is already the case in much of our military policy.

Two possible new and important changes in foreign aid philosophy merit mention, for if they become trends they will change our relationship with at least some underdeveloped countries and, in doing so, will alter the roles as well as the viewpoints of some youths:

a. It may be that our population will not consume at the rate necessary to keep unemployment at acceptably low levels, if there are both increased productivity and a much-enlarged unskilled, low-paid, young, working-age population. In such a crisis, the government might overcome its present inability to transcend conventional standards of participation in the economy and choose instead to stimulate it by buying excess goods and giving them to underdeveloped nations.

b. Calculated, all-out development of particular nations or regions to make them showcases in the economic cold war might well be a new form of aid used by both the United States and the USSR in the next two decades. To limit the demands from less-favored underdeveloped nations, and to ensure that our programs go according to plans, the nations enjoying our large-scale largess would operate very much as satellites, politically and economically controlled from the United States. Strong-man governments would make such programs easier to implement, and such governments are likely in nations struggling to accumulate capital.

To retain their independence, many underdeveloped nations probably will continue to try to play off East against West. But the possibility of rapid growth, of fame for the leadership and prestige to the nation, may overcome this present tactic and make particularly appealing the externally managed, packaged development program. This approach is not likely to develop rapidly for many reasons, not the least of which is the limited experience the United States and the USSR have had at this kind of social development program.

All in all, the impact of the underdeveloped nations on the economies, ethics, and military stability of the world will be serious indeed during these next twenty years. Robert Heilbroner sums it up: "Ahead lies a long gantlet through which rich and poor, favored and disfavored alike must pass; and in that period of trial it is less likely that the poor will falter who have their lives at stake than the rich who may fear for their way of life." (2)

References

1. Heilbroner, Robert L., *The Great Ascent*. New York: Harper & Row, 1963, p. 169.
2. *Ibid.*, p. 183.

Supplementary References

Asher, Robert E., *et al.*, *Development of the Emerging Countries*. Washington, D.C.: Brookings Institution, 1952.

Lerner, Max, *America as a Civilization.* New York: Simon and Schuster, 1957.

Mead, Margaret, "The Underdeveloped and the Overdeveloped," *Foreign Affairs,* Vol. 41, No. 1, Council on Foreign Relations, Inc., New York, October 1962, pp. 78–89.

Possible Non-military Scientific Developments and Their Potential Impact on Foreign Policy Problems of the United States, Stanford Research Institute, prepared at the request of the Committee on Foreign Relations, United States Senate, 86th Congress, 1st Session, September 1959.

The United Nations Development Decade: Proposals for Action, Report of the Secretary-General, Department of Economic and Social Affairs, United Nations, New York, 1962.

CHAPTER

6

DEVELOPED NATIONS

FOR THE same reasons that we have examined developing nations' trends, we need to attend to trends and circumstances in the developed nations over the next twenty years. Youth here will be deeply affected by occupational and cultural opportunities in these countries; by their economic and cultural impact on us; by their growing ability to set the pace and modulate our beliefs and values.

The very capacities and processes which define nations as "developed" also make it impossible to discuss them in general without being vague about their future trends and circumstances. The system of relationships among developed nations is extraordinarily viable, but it is also subject to enormous shifts in emphasis and direction over short periods of time—as the postwar histories of Germany, Russia, and Japan demonstrate. The power implicit in their material riches and their far-flung communications nets which quickly distribute words, decisions, finances, and feelings mean that more personalities and events can be decisive for each developed country's future than can be so in the underdeveloped nations, where capital and communications are scarce.

Whatever the changes in the other developed nations, they will be at least as momentous as changes in the United States over the next twenty years. The changes in other developed countries will be caused by and will cause circumstances similar to those in this country.

Generally speaking, Europe and the United States will face many of the same trends in problems and opportunities. For example, pressures in this country toward experiments with metropolitan districts and regional methods for dealing with urban problems will be paralleled by pressures toward a deeper formal interdependence of nations, as now represented by the European Economic Community. Another example: the shift to cybernation has already begun in Europe and the USSR, for the same reasons as in the United States.

The trend definitely will be in the direction of European unity—ideologically, economically, militarily, and perhaps politically. Some strengthening of ties between the United States and Europe, and between the United States and some other developed nations comprising the Western Bloc, will occur. Some evolution of the Atlantic Community is very likely. (1) But for the next decade and more, European nations will be too preoccupied with working out close relationships among themselves to take on the huge added complication of closely incorporating the United States with its different values, perspectives, and styles of operation. As the Director of the Center for International Affairs of Harvard University, Robert R. Bowie, put it in a radio discussion:

The difficulty, though, is that we're going to go through a period of perhaps a decade of tension based on the fact that

Europe feels itself to be a reality. It feels like a grouping that is entitled to be dealt with as an equal, and yet it hasn't achieved the degree of cohesion or the instruments or the institutions which enable it to act effectively as a unit in world affairs, in defense, or in other respects. The result is going to be that the United States is going to feel more frequently exasperated because there's no Europe to deal with, although Europe insists on being dealt with as an equal. The Europeans are going to feel exasperated because the United States doesn't deal with them with the equality which they feel entitled to by reason of their returned self-confidence and revival. If we can get through this period without excessive friction or impatience, we have a good prospect of having the vision of partnership which the present Administration has espoused work out as a perfectly feasible kind of relation, but the trick is going to be to get from here to there. (2)

The same is probably true for Europe's relations with the underdeveloped nations and with Japan, Canada, New Zealand, and others.

A major consequence of the growth of a European viewpoint, and the economic, political, and military power to emphasize it, will be a gradual reduction of the United States' status and role as the pre-eminent power of the West. Our support of the UN will be strongly challenged by some of our population, as its decisions often will conflict with our national interests. These decisions will result not only from communist intransigence, but from the more profound differences that will arise between us and our allies as our economies and power politics vary in purpose.

The world-wide political-economic differentiation between the Eastern and Western Blocs will decrease as Europe becomes an independent political and economic power center, and as the USSR becomes a richer, consumer-oriented society more concerned with and competent to pursue domestic growth and political-economic competition, and more able to use (or, at least, tolerate) considerable dissent, especially from its present college generation.

During this period communist China either will have collapsed or, more likely, will be developing into a military and industrial nation pursuing goals and using means sometimes alarmingly different from those pursued by the Western nations, including Russia. (The collapse of China would be one of those events so rich in alternative and unanticipated consequences that little would be gained by exploring that contingency here, especially in terms of its significance as a background factor in youth development.) If China grows, areas of common interest probably will increase between Russia and Europe and the United States. The USSR will come to trade much more than at the present time with the highly developed Western Bloc nations. She will also compete more strenuously for the underdeveloped nation market as her productive capability increases, especially if arms control and disarmament measures permit reductions in her military investment and increases in civilian productivity. All in all, the chances are good that over time the USSR will decrease as a direct military threat to the Western Bloc and increase as a political, economic, and social challenge.

However, Stanley Hoffman warns that:

. . . while this process takes place we are obviously in for some very tense moments, in part because this process would involve a destruction or disintegration of the unity of the Soviet bloc. The ultimate vision of this pluralistic world is so much the opposite from what the Soviet Union wishes that it is not going to adjust to it easily. And secondly we have been so used to being the dominant power in the competition of the Western side, that even though the direction in which the world is going is one which ultimately is exactly what we should want and what we have wanted, we also have a whole painful process of readjustment to go through. So these are not going to be very pleasant years, not any more pleasant than the last fifteen have been. (3)

Mutually rewarding joint economic growth programs will increase. Some will be under government auspices, but many will involve a growing number of United States and foreign businesses. These multinational businesses will tend to become internationally oriented. This does not mean that their national allegiances will disappear but that ideas and feelings about national allegiance, sovereignty, and so on, will become more differentiated and less a matter of reflex chauvinism. The traditional state of mind of the scientist, with his allegiance to and working ideal of knowledge as the possession of man rather than of states (with the emotional problems and satisfactions this produces), will be to some extent analogously experienced by nonscientists in the business and institutional world that spans the developed nations.

Problem-oriented, rather than nation-oriented, viewpoints will be emphasized among experts and bureaucrats from various nations working together, but at a distance, on the same tasks as a result of the widespread and frequent use of telephone, teletype, and facsimile, via the inexpensive service provided by satellite communications.

However, the United States will not always find its economic and political interests compatible with those nations who now comprise the Western Bloc. As productive capabilities increase here and abroad and as products become more similar in function and quality, competitive pressures will increase. Arrangements will proliferate between governments and producers to stimulate, or inhibit forms of competition, depending on the national interest. Political actions in these areas will be influenced, of course, by the viewpoints and interests of these multinationally oriented businessmen. In the process some national industries will decline while others grow; this will complicate further the problems of matching and meshing manpower.

As the European Common Market, including England, becomes an effective instrument of trade and political barriers *within* the market are lessened, barriers between the Common Market and other nations of the world will probably increase. The United States, unilaterally, will be in a less and less advantageous position, not only with respect to trade, but also with respect to exerting its influence upon the Common Market members apropos economic, political, and military policy regarding the Soviet bloc. As can be seen from past experience, trade and economics often set the outer limits for political and military policies. This is not only the case in Europe, but has also been the case in the United States. (4)

It is by no means unlikely that during the next twenty years the United States will seek to cope with the growing economic power of the European Common Market and that of the USSR bloc by establishing its own common market, involving perhaps Canada, Japan, Australia, Mexico, and other Latin American states.

Student exchange among all developed nations, and especially the number of United States students studying in other countries, will increase greatly as recent improvements in language training and in other subjects taught in our schools begin to bear fruit, and as a larger number of American parents live and work outside the United States. The exchange, however, will be chiefly among superior students, for they will have the linguistic and cultural prerequisites and the subject-matter competence to make the transfer mutually rewarding.

There will be many opportunities for closer meshing of cultural and educational activities, with more joint development programs in both basic and applied science and engineering, and probably in the arts and humanities as well. In particular, major multinational efforts in the 1970's will be likely in space exploration and oceanography, including the establishment of small undersea colonies.

If seasonal weather forecasts improve substantially, economic and humanitarian motives are very likely to produce new international cooperative arrangements. Foreknowledge of weather extremes (and, consequently, of harvest size) will make crop and fuel allocation matters for international negotiation and planning rather than matters chiefly keyed to domestic or private economic perspectives, or worked out when events overtake ignorance. Such foreknowledge will also be a potent weapon in economic warfare.

Of special importance for viewpoints and values in the United States will be the extensive use by other highly developed nations of government intervention and over-all coordination to meet the labor, leisure, and education challenges of the next two decades. There will be lessons and discomforts for us in the means they use to meet their futures. There will be failures resulting from too much government intervention and we will learn from these. Their successes will add to our ideas of how these tasks might be accomplished and to our feelings of insecurity and frustration when these successes challenge our beliefs and operating styles. It is entirely possible that the methods used will both encourage and force us into similar methods more rapidly than would be the case if there were no examples of democratic societies using greater government powers than we regularly do, and if we find that through the use of these powers others are accomplishing necessary changes faster than we. Increased communication and face-to-face experiences, especially among the decision-makers and leaders of opinion, will facilitate this awareness and will bring these matters home much faster and in more detail than is now the case.

There will be the lurking threat that, pressed or panicked, we and other democratic nations will misuse these government powers and, as we have too frequently in the past, that we will use totalitarian means to "preserve" democracy. How likely it is that we will misuse these powers depends on how hard we are pressed and on how easily we panic in the face of the deep problems we are likely to encounter.

References

1. "A New Europe?" *Daedalus,* American Academy of Arts and Sciences, Vol. 93, No. 1, Boston, Mass., Winter 1964.

2. Bowie, Robert R., "United States Foreign Policy: Its Limits and Possibilities," *Daedalus on the Air,* American Academy of Arts and Sciences, Boston, 1963, pp. 14–15.

3. Hoffman, Stanley, "United States Foreign Policy: Its Limits and Possibilities," *Daedalus on the Air,* American Academy of Arts and Sciences, Boston, 1963, pp. 16–17.

4. *National Economic Effectiveness: The Role of U. S. Foreign Economic Policy in World Conflict.* Menlo Park, Calif.: Stanford Research Institute Project 3711, February 1962, p. 61. (Prepared for the Office of the Director, Office of Emergency Planning, Washington, D.C.)

Supplementary References

Drucker, Peter R., "Japan Tries for a Second Miracle," *Harper's,* Vol. 226, No. 1354, March 1963, pp. 72-78.

Herter, Christian A., *Toward an Atlantic Community.* New York: Harper & Row, Inc., 1963.

Kraft, Joseph, *The Grand Design: From Common Market to Atlantic Partnership.* New York: Harper & Row, 1962.

Lerner, Daniel, "Will European Union Bring about Merged National Goals?" *The Annals of the American Academy of Political and Social Sciences,* Vol. 348, July 1963, pp. 34-45.

Lichtheim, George, *The New Europe—Today and Tomorrow.* New York: Praeger, 1963.

Stillman, Edmund, and William Pfaff, *The New Politics: America and the End of the Postwar World.* New York: Coward-McCann, Inc., 1961.

Stoessinger, John, *The Might of Nations.* New York: Random House, Inc., 1962.

CHAPTER

7

PEACE AND WAR

THE POSSIBILITIES for peace or war are included here because they will affect the aspirations, actions, and justifications for these actions, of youth and their adult guides. Not everyone will be affected in the same way, any more than they are now. Some will find in the threat of war the inspiration for commitment to socially positive tasks; others will use the threat as a justification for living in the present; still others will repress their sense of or be indifferent to the general world context. But as general education improves and as there is increasing awareness at home of the growing dependency of our goals on those of other nations, peace and war will loom as cogent and salient issues for a somewhat greater portion of the population, thereby modifying plans made for youth and their plans for themselves.

It is most unlikely that many of those who now perceive the world as facing the possibility of annihilation will see it as consistently and substantially free of that threat over the next ten years, or even twenty. There doubtless will be shifts in weapons systems, and there probably will be significant attempts at implementing some arms control and disarmament measures later in this decade. These will be slow and halting, at least at first, as the parties learn what the implications of each step are for their national interests—economic as well as military. During this time it is highly likely that there will be imagined or real threats to national interests growing out of shifts in or restraints on weapons systems and their deployment. World-wide political unrest and political-economic revolutions favoring the interests of one major power or another will result in anxious explorations (partially public) of the consequences of using or threatening to use various kinds of weapons in these peripheral contests. Clandestine and guerrilla warfare may well increase, along with the use of both lethal and nonlethal chemical and biological agents to do everything from defoliating food-bearing trees to assassinating leaders. More countries may have nuclear weapons. This will increase the opportunities for small nations to indulge in escapades which dangerously entangle the great powers. China most likely will become more potent and disruptive, though the focus of her antagonism may become more diffused.

Over all, there will continue to be deep differences of opinion as to how threatening the world situation is and how devastating the existing weapons are. At any given stage of political-military affairs, there will be highly esoteric arguments for and against the military *status quo,* arguments demonstrating our security and counterarguments demonstrating the imminence, or at least the plausibility, of annihilation. There is no good reason to suppose that during the next ten years weapons will be reduced to the point where essentially all citizens will be convinced that war, if it should come, would not be catastrophic.

The type of adults and adolescents who now worry about these matters will continue to do so, with some increase in the proportion of youth and young adults who truly grasp the nature of the factors involved and are deeply preoccupied with the issues.

Both informed and emotionally based actions and ideas about what should be done, either about the presumed threat from weapons or about enhancing security through weapons, will probably become more intense in that part of the population which attends to these issues. But there is no reason to believe that preoccupation with these matters will spread through most sectors of the population. Rather, it is more likely that the gulf between the concerned and the indifferent will increase as the general public becomes more isolated from the complex details of the issues. Indeed, even as now, a goodly portion of well-educated youths and adults will continue to feel too frustrated and inadequate in the face of these complexities (and secrecies) to make a continuing and active effort to understand the issues and to try to influence their outcomes. However, the peace movement as such probably will gain recruits and activists, so long as world events do not make it more difficult to argue the insufficiency of weapons and war as the road to peace.

It is possible, of course, that perceived national security needs, combined with other national and international frustrations and threats, will encourage the United States to become a garrison state. An important expression of this state of mind could be a large fallout shelter program, including mandatory training for all citizens.

The balance in favor of extensive arms control and disarmament could be shifted quickly and radically by the accidental or deliberate explosion of a nuclear weapon which destroys a city but does not initiate an all-out war. (As the major nuclear nations develop virtually invulnerable retaliatory weapons under the ocean and in the air, the need to strike back quickly and totally will disappear. Such invulnerability will mean that those initiating an attack could not destroy the capability for a later retaliatory response. Therefore, the potential retaliator can take his time in responding to make sure where the attack came from and that it was not accidental. This capability for delayed response will exist in both the United States and the USSR by the late 1960's.) A "city-killing" disaster will become more likely if less experienced and less responsible nations (and even private parties) come to possess a few nuclear weapons. This development is mentioned because, while it is not likely, it is possible in the years ahead; it is possible at any time; the horror and terror generated may be sufficient to provide the political context in many nations for all-out disarmament or arms control programs.

References

Millis, Walter, *et al., World Without War.* New York: Washington Square Press, Inc., 1961.

Waskow, Arthur I., *The Limits of Defense.* New York: Doubleday & Company, Inc., 1962.

SECTION

11

*Conditions Subject
to Considerable Influence
by Youth Developers*

CHAPTER

8

MARRIAGE, SEX, AND THE FAMILY

BARRING depressions, the strong tendency toward early marriage will probably continue. According to the U. S. Census Bureau, in recent years about 40 per cent of girls marrying were twenty years old or less, and about half of these have had children while still in their teens. As long as youth have the money, this trend is likely to continue, especially for those not going on to professional careers or college. Time on their hands, a sense of footlessness and "nothing better to do," a growing belief that the government will care for them one way or another—all will contribute to this trend. The tendency toward earlier pubescence in girls also will encourage it, as will the continuing social pressures to hurry youth into adult behavior while discouraging them from expressing it as long as they remain adolescent, i.e., single.

It is certainly possible that because of large numbers, lack of skill, and technological change, an unprecedented number of youths entering (or trying to enter) the work force will not be able to earn incomes adequate to make marriage attractive. It is also possible that the government will subsidize this large consumer market and at the same time keep it out of the competitive job market by paying youths to stay in school or to work at government-supported projects which use unskilled labor. Since, in the nature of our political processes, this is more likely to happen after serious economic difficulties arise for youth, there may be a temporary slackening of early marriages during the hiatus.

The pattern of college and graduate-school marriages very probably will continue, especially if students find opportunities to earn extra income as preprofessionals or skilled apprentices in intern and training programs instituted by skill-starved businesses and government.

If inexpensive oral contraceptives are available, they may also reduce the marriage rate. However, where marriage is the result of pregnancy the success of this deterrent would depend on the extent to which males would risk being trapped into marriage by females who claimed they had used the contraceptive when they hadn't. (The likely development of male oral contraceptives would redress the balance.)

But the availability of cheap, effective oral contraceptives certainly will accelerate changes in values about the relationships between couples quite aside from their marriage plans. Readily available contraception; high physical mobility and a larger urban geography to be easily mobile in; adult-mimicking social behavior in adolescents and preadolescents; a consumer-oriented economy with its explicit approval of self-indulgence; splintered value systems, accompanied for some by the persisting threat of war; the declining role of the family as the behavior-constraining and behavior-defining

agency for youth; additional emotional insecurities suf-
fered by underprivileged youth when jobs for them become more scarce; the alienation of some of the more
privileged youth, and their turning to intense personal
relationships as an answer—all of these factors will encourage extensive experimenting with premarital sex.

It is also likely that these factors will encourage
sexual experimenting among more adults—especially
among those already envious of the freedom of youth.
Such adult behavior will itself reinforce similar behavior
in youth.

There will be no adequate set of agreed-on goals and
purposes which society—and thereby parents—expects
the adolescent to meet. Spokesmen for society will vari-
ously expect adolescents to: (a) prepare for a job or get
one; (b) be a highly responsive consuming market; (c)
behave like adults without being accepted as adults;
(d) do not as parents do, but as they say. Ambivalence,
frustration, misunderstanding, and indifference will be
typical responses of the different generations to one
another. Older children and adolescents are turning
increasingly for direction and understanding to their
peers or to adult cynosures who act in ways the peer
group approves.

Other adult and peer influences probably will grow
and affect larger proportions of the youth population.
At the same time, pressures will continue on parents to
arrange their lives and their children's to mesh with
whatever life styles are conveyed by the mass media
and opinion-makers to whom they listen and respond.
In most cases, parents will not find in these powerful
"reality definers" and style-setters any consistent guides
to conscientious and incisive parental behavior and
standards.

With improvements in primary and secondary school curricula and teaching methods many youths will become more familiar with the larger world (at least, with science and technology) and often more sophisticated about it than their parents. Frequently they will reason more accurately on more complex matters than their parents can. Additionally, the inability of many parents to deal consistently or meaningfully, in terms of their values, with the rapidly changing world (both the big one and their children's), or their indifference in the face of their offsprings' enthusiasm or despair about the world, will for many youth emphasize the older generation's incapacity to deal with many of the basic needs of the younger.

This state of affairs is really not parallel to that which existed between immigrants and their American-born children. The immigrant parents lacked sureness about their place in the new world, but frequently they held strong values which they tried to impose on their young. Compared to immigrant parents, many parents today feel at home in this world and that, one way or another, they are of it. But they don't know what values toward it to urge on their children.

Although the relative influence of parents on the behavior and guidance of their children will continue to decline for the most part, some youths will continue to look to their parents for guidance, and parental influence will not decline equally in all socioeconomic groups. There will probably be more opportunities, as society increases in size and complexity, for religious and ideologically-based groups to encourage in their followers —parents and youth alike—behavior patterns more or less at variance with the prevailing styles of those parts of society which surround and interpenetrate these subgroups. Doubtless some of these groups will make attempts to substitute discipline and asceticism for what is perceived as self-indulgence and aimlessness, and doubtless they will have some success. However, present evidence suggests that what parents believe and do will not always determine what their children do, even in the more disciplined and sterner groups and even when the youths claim the same values as their parents.

In the future some parents will be surer of their place in life, some less sure. The lessening age difference between youth and parents; the growing opportunity, at least in part, to "catch up" with or surpass their children through adult education; the indifference of many youth to the new world, its values and complexities, will blur some old differences between parents and youth and emphasize others. Indeed, for some youth the family will continue to be a crucial source of emotional support, a basic jumping-off place, an oasis.

At the very least, then, there will be greater ambivalence in the relationship between youth and parents; it will be a more difficult task for parents to guide their children wisely and well. This state of affairs gives every indication of intensifying over the next two decades as adults, adolescents, and children struggle to find themselves in their own generational milieu and in relation to one another.

Additional factors will tend to contribute to trends in the relations between the generations. Work-camp jobs for the unskilled and schooling opportunities in distant places for the career-oriented adolescent will also encourage physical separation. At the same time, increasing ease and lessening cost of transportation will facilitate both separation and opportunities for reunion. If this separation eases the between-generation emotional problems of adolescence and early maturity, it may strengthen other parent-offspring relationships. Indeed, under the pressures discussed above, and given the relative ease of reunion, this pattern of physical separation between the generations may well become far more prevalent than it is today.

The continuing shift of population from rural to urban centers will continue to break the remaining family roots of the city immigrants. While family visiting during vacations will be easier and, as now, popular, physical separation of the urban and rural parts of the family will undoubtedly lead to divergence of values and life styles.

In a growing portion of families there will be a new recognition that sooner or later one may be unemployed, or, at best, that one's job will change in content and perhaps in employer, and that retraining and physical uprooting are likely for both parent-worker and youth worker-to-be. School dropouts and unmotivated, unskilled, late adolescents will become more of a financial and emotional strain on their families and themselves as jobs grow scarcer. Apprehension, enthusiasm, or indifference to these states of affairs will vary in various occupational strata. The extent to which the generations share or differ in their viewpoints on these matters will further separate some families and bring others together.

Greater leisure time for some adults will not, in many cases, provide more opportunities for family "togetherness," since school hours and school days are likely to increase. Moreover, relations between parents may alter significantly as they spend more time together or devise ways to stay apart. It is also likely that there will be more day nurseries and baby-sitting help as the proportion of unskilled, unemployed women increases and as more older women skilled in such activities establish these services. This, in turn, will make it possible for skilled women and some of the unskilled who now must stay home with their youngsters to have at least some time free for careers or service out of the house. Changes in child-raising patterns and in mother–child and husband–wife relations will naturally follow. Perhaps young girls will find in their active mothers a model for behavior sufficiently strong and attractive to lead them to aspire to careers beyond marriage and motherhood. The reapportionment for family members of time together and the changes in activities of wives and adolescents outside the home will probably profoundly affect how each member of the family defines his or her dependence on and autonomy from the others. The traditional role each plays with respect to the others in the family context will thereby be changed even more. The family, which traditionally has been society's fundamental institution, will accelerate its transformation into yet unclear forms and functions.

Supplementary References

Bell, Norman W., and Ezra F. Vogel, eds., *A Modern Introduction to the Family*. New York: The Free Press of Glencoe, Inc., 1960.

Cohen, Albert K., *Delinquent Boys: The Culture of the Gang*. New York: The Free Press of Glencoe, Inc., 1955.

Douvan, Elizabeth, and Carol Kaye, *Adolescent Girls*. Survey Research Center, Institute for Social Research, University of Michigan, Ann Arbor, Mich., 1957.

Erhmann, W., *Premarital Dating Behavior*. New York: Holt, Rinehart, & Winston, 1959.

Goode, William J., "Family Disorganization" in Robert K. Merton and Robert A. Nisbet, eds., *Contemporary Social Problems*. New York: Harcourt, Brace, & World, Inc., 1961.

Hechinger, Grace and Fred M. Hechinger, *Teen-Age Tyranny*. New York: William Morrow & Co., 1963.

Mead, Margaret, "Problems of the Late Adolescent and Young Adult," *Golden Anniversary White House Conference on Children and Youth,* Department of Health, Education and Welfare. Washington, D.C.: U. S. Government Printing Office, 1960, pp. 3–12.

Sirjamaki, John, *The American Family in the Twentieth Century.* Cambridge, Mass.: Harvard University Press, 1953.

Withey, Stephen B., and Elizabeth Douvan, *A Study of Adolescent Boys.* Survey Research Center, Institute for Social Research, University of Michigan, Ann Arbor, Mich., 1956.

———, B. Foster, and P. Billingsley, *A Study of Boys Becoming Adolescents.* Survey Research Center, Institute for Social Research, University of Michigan, Ann Arbor, Mich., 1960.

CHAPTER

9

EDUCATION

CHANGING PERSPECTIVES

ONLY GRADUALLY, and chiefly at the occupationally elite level of society, will it become evident that the educational requirements for productive and meaningful lives will require profound changes in the procedures, substance, and spirit of the educative processes, beginning at least as early as the primary grades and continuing throughout life. Values and behavior that emphasize and comfortably mesh commitment to task; flexibility in learning, unlearning, and relearning; constructive attitudes toward and effective use of more hours of leisure, and so on, cannot be taught just at the college level, or probably even as late as high school; and they cannot be taught by teachers who do not share these values. They probably must be learned in childhood and then modified throughout life as an active learning experience.

On a national scale this deep change in the philosophy and content of education can only come gradually as the appropriate influential institutions develop sufficient sense of where they should go and what needs to be done to get there. More research will be necessary to determine what needs to be done and which of the many ways explored are the most effective and economical. These studies will be evaluated and re-evaluated, if only because there will be partisan argument about their meanings. Then the results, good, bad, and indifferent, will have to be understood and accepted by those who must act on them to alter the complex institutions of teaching. This will require changes in the viewpoints of Congress, state legislatures, teachers' colleges and schools of education, public school systems, PTA's, taxpayers, and, not least, the teacher. After this the changes will have to be applied. Still later, the products will begin to move into the adult world.

Then, too, various powerful and vocal groups will slow the rate of the inevitable and necessary commitment of truly large-scale Federal Government investments for educational support. In the words of the Carnegie Corporation:

Race, religion, federal "control" of education, division of the spoils among the states, the purposes for which aid should be given—each of these issues has figured as an effective deterrent to passage since the beginning of federal aid legislation. But whereas in the past one issue, or a combination of two or three, has been sufficient to block legislation, now *all* of them are involved in the controversy, which leads . . . [to] . . . an extremely dim view of the possibilities of early passage of general aid. (1)

Gradual, erratic, disparate as these changes in education will be, they nevertheless will be great over the next twenty years.

ELEMENTARY SCHOOL AND
HIGH SCHOOL DEVELOPMENTS

More intensive experiments will be conducted to determine better ways to use live teachers, team teaching, and teachers' aides; programed and self-paced instruction and audio-visual aids. The results will be applied gradually in more primary and secondary schools, particularly those whose student bodies are relatively privileged. To the extent that these methods for learning depend on self-starting and self-sustaining motives, they will be more easily and successfully applied to these privileged youth. Then, too, such experiments need strong support from parents, teachers, and school administrations. Generally, these conditions are more likely to be found in the wealthier communities where parents, by virtue of their socioeconomic position, are more likely to have favorable attitudes toward teaching experiments and toward providing their children with the best opportunity to compete successfully for college acceptance. As a rule, too, the more imaginative and experimental teachers and administrators will find their way to these better schools because of their superior working environments, higher pay, and greater status.

In the better primary and secondary schools the more talented students will be increasingly allowed to blur the boundaries between school years by dealing with subject matter according to their ability rather than by age or grade. Until programed instruction is used and administered more imaginatively, and until teaching and administrative staffs have physical resources and personal commitment sufficient to deal with the coming school population explosion better than they deal with today's situation, self-paced study at least for the superior student (including such as advanced placement and honors programs) and team teaching are likely to be the two most widespread changes instituted within and among schools.

Another change will grow from the likelihood that all school levels from primary through university will move toward a twelve-month operation. Greater variety of subject matter and increasing numbers of students will encourage this change. Vacations for some students (particularly the preprofessionals) will be shortened, and not all students and teachers will have their vacations at the same time. Staggered vacations will both ease the teacher's work load and permit a more even distribution of demand on increasingly overloaded recreational facilities. It will also encourage a more even distribution over the year of the (longer) vacation periods of working parents.

The significance of the junior high school and its future trend seems to be summed up by Margaret Mead:

The junior high school has become a forcing ground for inappropriate and socially maladjusted attitudes in both boys and girls, laying the basis for hostility to females on the boys' part and, on the girls' part, grasping pressure toward marriage combined with contempt for males. Although these deficiencies of the junior high school are widely recognized, the attractiveness of using new junior high schools as a quick solution to the population pressures on the school system makes it probable that the evils of the junior high school will increase rather than decrease during the next decade. (2)

At the same time, it is likely that more school systems will experiment with graded or ungraded arrangements which eliminate the junior high. The shortage of good teachers who are willing to teach junior high, more flexible teaching and administrative schemes, and the problems Mead emphasizes will add incentives to try other arrangements.

PROGRAMED INSTRUCTION

The potential flexibility and utility of programed instruction seems very great indeed, and it is being used and will be used imaginatively and fruitfully. (3) However, little of this potential is likely to be exploited to the fullest during the next decade or so. Wilbur Schramm, in his summary of the present and foreseeable state of programed instruction, has this to say:

a. Although the research gives us little reason to be satisfied with the theories and the standards of today's programing, and every reason to believe that it will be possible some day to make programs vastly more effective than today's programs, nevertheless programed instruction shows signs of hardening, partly under commercial pressure, into a fixed and mechanical technology, with theories and procedures taken for granted.

b. Although programed instruction has within it the potential to turn the attention of education and educational research more intensively and productively than ever before to the processes by which humans learn, there is very little sign that it is being used productively to test theories of human learning or theories of cognitive process, or to enlighten the teacher concerning the process by which she teaches.

c. Although programed instruction is essentially a revolutionary device, in that it has the potential to help free man from some of his bondage—the waste of human resources where there are no teachers or where people cannot go to school; the waste of time and talent where all students are locked into the same pace, and all teachers into the same routine; the tyranny of tradition which permits the study of a certain topic to begin only at a certain age, and expects a student to accomplish only so much as a questionable test of his ability says he can do; and the inadequacy of outmoded and inadequate curricula—despite this, programed instruction is very slow to rise to such a revolutionary potential. (4)

Thus, unless otherwise noted, subsequent discussions of the role of teaching machines and programed instruction assume that, for a number of years at least, their popular application, with notable exceptions, will be to facilitate a relatively pedestrian level of factual learning and as an adjunct to today's typical modes of educational administration.

Of course, experiments with programed learning, teaching machines, and related aids are and will be conducted in run-of-the-mill and deprived schools in the hope that these devices will overcome the limits imposed on live teachers working with large classes. Funds for such experiments will be progressively easier to find, but it will take time to train staffs to teach effectively by these means, to gain the active support of parents, and to generate motives in the students which will be rewarded by the fact of learning correctly. (Doubtless, studies focused on expanding the variety of motives that teaching machines can stimulate and reward will be under way.) But unless the government and the educational establishment make an all-out effort to provide funds and direction for changing the school system as a whole, the rate of introduction of these methods will be slowest in precisely those schools whose students have relatively the most to gain through the substitution of good programed learning for overworked or mediocre teachers.

Possibly by the 1970's the situation will have reached a sufficiently critical state for the government to take the lead on the required scale. By then, the educa-

immediate future. The formal organizational complexity is great and traditions are extensive and vigorously protected, in the maze of viewpoints and institutions influencing and controlling teachers, school administrators, teachers' colleges, schools of education, accreditation agencies, school boards, and primary school, secondary school, and college relations. Changes in the substance and conduct of live teaching required to produce a majority of citizens capable of living full and meaningful lives in tomorrow's world will take many years to accomplish.

CURRICULA

In the next twenty years, especially in the better schools, there will be major improvements in the curricula for secondary and, to a lesser degree, primary schools. Mathematics and natural science texts and teaching already show marked improvements because of national stress on the physical sciences, because they are ethically neutral subjects, and because many aspects of these subjects lend themselves with relative ease to programed instruction methods. Improvement in other subject matter will be more gradual; it is already more or less under way in such subjects as biology, English, and the behavioral sciences. But in areas where the subject matter can be more controversial and its interpretation less bound by "facts," changes in curricula will be slower. Differences in interpretation and emphasis among experts preparing the subject matter and the persistence of conventional viewpoints about the material in question in the communities and institutions that will finally choose whether or not to use the new materials, will be responsible for this relative slowness to change.

ORGANIZATIONAL TRENDS AT
THE COLLEGE LEVEL

Because they face the same problems as the primary and secondary schools, colleges will only gradually make important improvements, and these will be uneven. Nevitt Sanford, editor of *The American College,* puts it this way:

The American college, and American institutions of higher learning generally, are embedded in our culture and in our society. They are expressive of persistent trends, and persistent conflicts, in the American value system, and they have a diversity of important functions in society. This means that fundamental or widespread change in the colleges can come about only when there is a shift of emphasis in our general system of values or when there is a change in our general societal processes. (6)

In the next twenty years higher education will be struggling with problems parallel to those facing the nation. Most important, the colleges and universities face an enormous population explosion. According to the Office of Education, the 4,200,000 students enrolled in the fall of 1962 are projected to increase by 24 per cent by 1965, by 67 per cent by 1970, and by 111 per cent by 1975! And these projections do not fully consider the potential enrollment of older adults returning in growing numbers for refresher courses, degrees, and for sheer intellectual and aesthetic stimulation during their increasing leisure time. (7)

Housing problems will themselves be enormous; Dr. Ernest V. Hollis, Director of College and University Administration in the Department of Health, Education and Welfare, estimates that two to three billion dollars will be needed annually for plant and equipment.

Administrative problems and experiments in administration will increase as more and more schools try to deal with a heterogeneous community of youth, many from backgrounds totally unfamiliar with the idea of higher learning and traditional university values. A growing portion of students will be well past the age of consent, many will be married, and many of the older students will be unsympathetic to rules designed to enforce the university's role *in loco parentis.*

Decentralization of administration and social control by dividing the student body into "houses" or "colleges" is one trend likely to gain in popularity. Another trend already well under way is the proliferation of satellite universities and junior colleges intended to absorb the less intellectually endowed and less career-focused students. The demand for school administrators will increase greatly. But in the absence of an adequate supply of good ones, and even in their presence, the ubiquitous computer will take on more and more of the paper work. In the days of the small college or university "individual student attention" was the minimum standard to which the administration aspired. However, the population explosion will make dim indeed the chances for implementing this standard. Under the combined impact of impracticability and the pressure to deal efficiently with paper work, the tendency will be to organize the administration of large universities around the rationalized procedures the computers make possible.

As the university population grows and becomes more heterogeneous, the university's ability to fulfill its role *in loco parentis* will lessen, and in some places disappear altogether. The rules in the books may become more explicit and precise for a few years, but enforcing them will become too tedious. Moreover, as parents come to see the large university as in reality a rather large community, with many of the more unsavory characteristics of the world outside the home, they will come less and less to expect the large university to substitute for themselves. Gradually, then, the large university or college will lose its protective role and the student will come to it expecting to be an autonomous individual, as he has been in most European universities.

However, European institutions of higher learning have had smaller student populations than ours do, and students came to them with a more intellectual and less socially oriented set of expectations about themselves and university life. Clearly, there will be emotional adjustments to be worked out in the big university environment as immature youths, in the midst of trying to find out who they are, are exposed to new ideas and to youths and older people from different backgrounds who espouse and live by many different values. For the emotionally secure student, this environment will be rich and stimulating. For the less secure youth, the sheer size and drive of the system may well push him into encapsulating himself among his own kind, thereby stripping the university experience of much enrichment beyond what he learns applicable to getting a job, or a spouse, or making "contacts." It is not impossible that married students will become mentors to the unmarried, and older students to the younger, married or single. By and large, the peer group will be the single most potent source of guidance. If the group is inspired by contact with ideas and a live teacher to spark real intellectual and emotional growth, this will be the chief mechanism available at large universities for learning and insight. For the great majority of the students, "higher education" probably will not add much more than it does now to their wisdom or deeper understanding.

Not all colleges and universities will be so big that they will face the problems and opportunities just speculated on. There will be a growing number of smaller satellite and independent two- and four-year colleges. Moreover, many of the better smaller colleges will restrict enrollment to about present levels. By keeping enrollments small these colleges will be able to skim off the best applicants. On the other hand, many of the applications to the two-year colleges and satellite institutions will be from those not acceptable at the central colleges; these institutions will be more likely to get the less desirable students and have less experienced and less talented faculties. Whether the latter trend is expressed this clearly will depend in part on how satisfied good students and good faculty will be with the environment of the big university. It is possible that later there may be a migration of better students and faculty away from the big institutions, analogous to the migration to the suburbs. This may be especially true in the humanities and the fine arts where large central physical facilities and laboratories are not prerequisites for training or original contributions as they are (and will be even more) in the natural and social sciences.

Moreover, the smaller institution will be able to continue to act *in loco parentis* and those students and their parents who prefer this relationship will seek out such institutions, even if the quality of the faculty and plant are not as imposing as those of the biggest universities.

TEACHING METHODS AT THE
COLLEGE LEVEL

Like primary and secondary schools, colleges will be pressed to develop and use audio-visual and related machines to improve the quality and amount of learning per unit time and to lessen the human teaching load as the student population increases. Both reasons will be influential, but the better institutions will emphasize the first, and the bigger or poorer schools, the second. The efflorescence of junior colleges and training schools will especially encourage this trend. There will not be enough good teachers to go around. Salaries offered in these schools will not be competitive with those of the richer schools; many classes will be too large for a good teacher to be truly effective; and much of their subject matter will be of the sort that can be relatively easily programed. These schools will have little choice but to amplify the quality and quantity of their staff by using audio-visual aids and teaching-machine programs.

As the college population grows, less and less of it will have opportunities for personal exposure to great live teachers, or even very much to mediocre ones (though vicarious exposure to great teachers will increase through closed-circuit TV and films). To be sure, this is already frequently the case as classes become larger and teachers more preoccupied with research. But with the increasing use of machine teachers and machine graders, attitudes toward the purposes of teaching and learning may be deeply affected. Important differences in perspective may develop between the viewpoints of those chiefly exposed to the facts-and-methods teaching machines and those relatively few also regularly exposed to the give-and-take of good live teachers.

Already the trend at each educational level is for only the most promising students to be truly exposed to an intimate teacher–student relationship. More and more, the relatively few good teachers will arrange their time and attention to mold and inspire the most interested and creative students through the give-and-take of conversations and essays involving the continuous, constructive "intellectual midwifery" that (insofar as we now know) only live teachers can provide. The vast remainder of the student body will learn in good part, but not exclusively, from closed-circuit television, films, and teaching machines, and will be tested automatically as well. Whether programed instruction will be able to provide the special influence of a good live teacher remains to be discovered. But the research needed is certain to take long and the implementation of any positive findings, still longer. Meanwhile, the growing size of the student body will increase the pressures to provide whatever education can be offered most of them via more primitive programs and machines.

QUALITY OF EDUCATION
AT ALL LEVELS

Over all, the difference in quality of education for average students will diminish and will average up rather than down, at least for factual learning—and, perhaps, for something more than that, if the number of better qualified instructors increases rapidly enough and as carefully planned teaching films and TV are used more broadly. But the difference between the learning experience of the ordinary student and the extraordinary one will be great.

However, it will become easier in future years to pay for a "higher" education. More and more subsidies will be available for both students and institutions. Two conditions are likely to stimulate the pace of giving: the continuing shortage of skilled people and the economic necessity to keep not-yet-skilled young people out of the competitive labor market. Support will be in the form of loans, outright gifts, and gifts contingent on occupational or service commitment to the fund's source, as is now the case with those receiving an advanced education at the expense of the military services and with those institutions doing contract research for the government and industry.

On balance, the next years will very likely see the beginnings of a pre-elite comprised of students who receive a special education at each level, which in turn will prepare them better than average students for special education at the next level. This has, of course, always been so to some extent. Education programs geared to the capabilities and career plans of students are already a trend, as evidenced by multiple "track" high schools and by two-year colleges which emphasize subjects congruent with the needs of local industry. But this trend will become more widespread and more urgent as the needs and standards for superior intellectual ability become ever higher in order to keep up with burgeoning social and technical problems and the exotic techniques available for trying to deal with them. This is not to say that the "elitist" trend will not be fought; it will be politically touchy indeed. Many schools will reject the elitist approach, and many will hide their compliance with it by hiring additional mediocre teachers to give the impression that all students receive equal attention. And, too, these students won't be defined as an "elite." Instead, they will more likely be described as especially dedicated and endowed potential "social servants" who, by virtue of their willingness to forego the pleasures of leisure, are to be compensated by a more intensive education which will also make them better social servants. The chances are good that a growing sense of the threat to social survival from growing social complexity will encourage this tendency to attend most solicitously to the most promising.

Over the next two decades all of these factors are likely to contribute to a state of mind in many adults and young people that unless one is highly talented, the "natural" way to learn is chiefly by depersonalized means. In large parts of the population it will also reinforce the view that the chief purpose of education is to provide the prerequisites for a well-paying job. Both views will be consonant with the general state of mind embracing or submitting to increasing rationalization.

OCCUPATION-ORIENTED
EDUCATION AT ALL LEVELS

Primary and secondary school training for work and for style of living would-be professionals, skilled technicians, and the unskilled will become more differentiated and focused than is now the case.

By and large, the most accomplished of the professionals (which increasingly will include management) will for the next two decades tend to work long hours, be time-oriented, require a deep and broad background in their fields, and need a lifelong ability to absorb fresh intellectual material. The youth aiming for such a career will begin to prepare for it early in life—certainly in high school, in most cases probably in primary school— if he is to compete successfully for access to the advanced education needed for professional success. Even though there will be more centers of higher education, the chances are that relatively few of these will be perceived as providing the best training and, at least in the physical sciences, probably only relatively few will be able to provide first-rate training. Top faculties in many of the most demanding and demanded professions will continue to be relatively scarce, as will be basic but costly equipment. The preprofessional student will also have to make a career choice in a broad but specific area (e.g., law vs. social science vs. physics) earlier than those not aspiring to a profession. He will be a "grind" in school rather than a seeker after "personal" experiences. Generally, he will feel more anxiety and be subject to more restraints on his time and activities which, compared to other youths, will hem him in and more intensively channel his activities. And if the youth has the talent, especially if he is a boy, he will be under increasing pressures to choose such a way of life in the national interest.

The technician (and more skilled jobs will become technical jobs as both standards and techniques become more demanding) will often, but not always, work shorter hours than the professional; be trained at a specialty; frequently expect to change specialty two or three times in his working life; and possess the social and psychological capabilities for learning a new specialty and for moving to another place to practice it. Since he will be well paid, he will also need training and values to make additional leisure time a rewarding social and private experience.

For many technical tasks it will not be necessary

to be as time-bound in outlook as the professional. Thus the student will be more casual about when he selects or is selected for education emphasizing job training; he will not have to make his general career choice as early or irrevocably as the preprofessional. He will be able to "play around" more throughout most of his schooling and, very possibly, his school hours will be fewer than the preprofessional's. He may also have more time to study nonvocationally oriented topics.

The unskilled will be unskilled because he will be relatively poorly educated, poorly motivated, and poorly incorporated into the values and behavior of the society of the intellect toward which we are headed. Thus he will also be poorly paid, whether he works short or long hours. A disproportionately large portion of the unskilled work force will be nonwhite, especially Negro, at least for the next two decades, simply because a disproportionately large portion of the nonwhite population will continue to receive education inadequate for more demanding jobs.

Not everybody will fall neatly into one of these three categories, of course, and the numbers in each category will not increase all at once. In particular, those planning creative careers in the fine arts and humanities will probably be exposed to and follow teachers and values very similar to those which now characterize these activities. The growing popularity of the fine arts and the growing number of potential artists will put greater strains on student-centered methods of teaching, and no doubt improvements will be introduced which use machines in ways similar to those now used in language teaching. But no great social forces applied through the formal educational system will drive the arts in the direction of mediocrity or mass production.

The humanities will also continue free from undue

pressure, though much of what is now taught in the large lecture hall will increasingly be taught by machine and film, and often taught much more effectively and vividly by these methods than by good scholars who are poor teachers. The proportion of younger students majoring in the liberal arts or taking many courses in them will probably decrease in the years ahead as the requirements for well-paying jobs demand more hours devoted to technical subjects. But the proportion of older people using their increased leisure time to study the fine arts and humanities will increase, in part because neither they nor the subjects will be oriented toward work.

Nevertheless, the three occupational categories described above will become sufficiently large and sufficiently important and different in social function and personal value so that those who follow these three paths will be exposed to different educations, each gradually evolving into different emphases in substance and values. These trends toward educational differentiation will parallel another type of differentiation which, by and large, will tend to reinforce the type of schooling characteristic of these three categories. Primary and secondary schools will continue to be good, mediocre, and bad depending on the economics, politics, and related factors associated with their geographic and ethnic location. The good schools will become better, being most responsive to the precursors of change and most able to take advantage of new methods to make the best of the changes anticipated. The mediocre schools, generally speaking, will improve, but not so much and not so all-inclusively, being subject to forces limiting foresight and funds and having to service many more students. The poor schools will probably become "rela-

tively" poorer compared to the others—at least until the
alienation and unemployment spawned by them produces a national crisis. But for some time yet, much will
tend to work against these schools, including public indifference and frequently hostility, as well as the impotence and misdirected motivations of the students and
their families.

SUPPLEMENTS TO THE INSTITUTIONALIZED EDUCATIONAL NETWORK

Teaching machines and programed instruction will extend the network of noninstitutionalized means for getting more education. Industry, business, unions, and
government will make more use of such methods to retain and broaden the training of their personnel. Supple-
mentary educational programs will be provided as
fringe benefits for both workers and management, and
increasingly such programs will include materials useful and available to their families as well. Experiments
are under way; programs in retraining for the disemployed will begin soon by programed instruction methods, when the subject matter, motivations, and ways of
learning of those to be retrained permit. Related research
presently under way should, in the years ahead, provide
a better basis for teaching those now very difficult or
impossible to retrain. Programed instruction will be used,
too, in the expanding adult education field, perhaps especially to teach leisure-time activities and to update the
training of women moving back into skilled occupations after child-raising.

Federal and state governments and private sources
will increasingly experiment with means for providing

the intellectually underendowed and the 8.3 million functionally illiterate with sufficient education to give them socially useful and self-respecting abilities. Progress will not be rapid, however. The task of developing teaching methods will be compounded by the necessity for finding meaningful tasks to be taught. For the growing population will provide a steady increase in the number of people with low IQ's simply because the distribution follows the normal curve in a heterogeneous population. IQ chiefly measures the capacity to manipulate symbols, and although opportunities for productive and rewarding lives will by no means be limited to those who can manipulate symbols well, the tendency will be —as we have said in many ways—for this ability to be increasingly in demand. While there will be growing efforts to deal with the underendowed, the main effort will for some years go to determining how and what to teach the better endowed who are untrained and unskilled.

The pressure will become very great indeed, especially in the next few years, for a radical revision and enlargement of the nation's vocational schools. The anticipated 7.5 million high school dropouts will critically enlarge the unskilled labor pool between now and 1970. Vocational training and retraining could radically reduce this profound threat to our economics and to our ethics of social responsibility. (8) At present, most vocational schools place emphasis on archaic topics unrepresentative of the nation's needs or job opportunities. (9) Widely applied revisions will not be easy or quick, however. Institutional inertia and interlocking interests will delay the amount and direction of changes here, as well as in the more general institution of education. In addition, there will be the substantial problem of finding teachers to teach the jobs that will be in demand; if the type of job is one with a good market, many of those able to teach it will be already employed, especially if skill is prerequisite. Then, too, the vocational training program will have to be tied into a job opportunity forecasting system and into a system offering the worker the mobility and financial support he will need to find a job if it is not to be found nearby. Without such forecasts, the numbers trained are not likely to match the jobs available.

GUIDANCE COUNSELING

There will be increasing emphasis on vocational guidance for both privileged and underprivileged youth, but adequate guidance will be difficult to provide and will for many years be least effective where most needed. Unless there are major changes in present operating conditions, qualified guidance personnel with the wide-ranging knowledge and (most important) with the influence to affect school curriculum planning will be in short supply for many years. It is estimated that only about three fifths of the recommended number of high school counselors. There are twice as many men as women counselors in secondary schools, a ratio which takes on special importance in the light of needed changes in occupations and avocations for women. (10)

Guidance will be especially important for technicians' jobs, since these will be the jobs most subject to change in a rapidly changing technology. Counselors will need detailed information about occupational opportunities two or ten years ahead and about anticipated labor markets abroad. But, as emphasized in the "Work" chapter of this book (pp. 117–19), it will be several more years, at least, before such information *may* be forthcoming.

Then, too, effective vocational guidance should be based on statistical knowledge about the characteristics of those who fail or succeed in particular occupations. But in the years ahead, job requirements and working conditions will change greatly—so greatly that different personal characteristics will be required in many jobs which may appear not to have changed because they will still carry the same old labels. (As a case in point, the frequent first-priority requirement today is that a scientist be able to get along on a team; in the old pattern, the scientist frequently was better off if he preferred to work alone.)

To counsel well requires knowledge about both candidate and job. But, increasingly the counselor is unlikely to have any real feel for the environment or spirit of the new occupations. Moreover, the high rate of technological change and rapid growth of specialized skills will mean that job types, variety, and qualifications will be changing relatively rapidly, especially in the skilled technical area. Such jobs will go to the less privileged and more average youth, but this group will be the most difficult for the counselor to reach in the more overcrowded, understaffed schools—which are also likely to be the least well organized to adjust their programs in the light of anticipated job changes.

Private enterprise and unions will probably contribute substantially to career guidance, as they now do through their in-service education programs. In this way, their own future needs will be well served.

EDUCATION FOR VALUES
AND PERSPECTIVES

In the years ahead there will be growing debate about the purposes of schooling beyond education for jobs or the national interest, and about how to educate to realize these purposes. Most fundamental will be the continuing and growing debate about the proper role of education in inculcating values and behavior appropriate to each of the occupational categories described above in a rapidly changing, complex, and contradictory world. Over the next twenty years this debate about the proper values for youth—who when they grow up will live in a world quite different from the world their elders know and can understand—will be carried on by parents and leaders, most of them trained by the past. It will be an intense debate and a partisan one, since we will continue to be unclear about the kind of world we want and what education we wish to emphasize for those ends. Unless we choose the garrison state as our preferred means for seeking preferred ends, this confusion will probably increase as our world becomes more complex. (For example, of renewed importance will probably be such issues as the virtues of saving and conserving versus those of spending and using up. On this and other issues, it will probably be socially desirable that different segments of the youth population hold different viewpoints when they become adults. These will be more fully subscribed to if they are cultivated during childhood and adolescence.) Implicit in the debate will be very difficult questions about the processes involved in teaching and changing values. For, although the understanding of the motivational and learning processes operating in the school context is considerable, it is still practically limited and will continue to be so until subtle studies providing additional understanding have been completed and evaluated.

At any rate, it is highly likely that, whatever else is involved, changing student perspectives will require teachers whose values are also appropriate to tomorrow's world. However, in general, primary and secondary school teachers for at least the next decade will continue to be recruited from backgrounds that stress lower-middle-class values of good behavior, "fitting in," political neutralism or conservatism, nationalism, reservations about alternative life styles, and conventional means for obtaining economic security. (11) They do not notably stress commitment to task, craftsmanship, independence, integrity, spontaneity, wide-ranging social and cultural tolerance and experiment, and attitudes encouraging the expectation of occupational changes. Thus, to considerable extent, the debate is likely to be an abstract one for most schools and students for many years.

One major focus of this debate will have to do with the extent and content of education for leisure and avocations. Conventional viewpoints on the virtues of work and pressures to remove educational "frills" in order to speed up the production of skillful workers will vie with the economic necessity to train youth in techniques for the voracious consumption of leisure-time products and to keep as many young people as possible out of the competitive work force. Stress on the need to teach the virtues of and means for the "creative" and "productive" use of leisure will increase, too.

As time goes on, this debate will be paralleled by many experiments in education for leisure—some specifically focused, some attempting to combine leisure and work. Margaret Mead suggests:

It should be possible to develop a new kind of vacation center which would provide for individuals of different ages—alone or as members of family groups—previews and test experiences of things they might do if they wished. Such a center would be a place where one could try out under expert tutelage the possibility of learning a new language, or dressmaking, or mechanics, or short story writing, or philosophy; it could provide the novice or the slightly trained student with two weeks of carefully planned laboratory experience in well-equipped, modern laboratories, with test experience in a field related to one in which the individual already had a growing interest—marine biology for the student who had some grounding in general biology, food chemistry for the student who had an elementary knowledge of general chemistry, and so on. (12)

Experiments such as the one Mead describes will involve education of the "how to do it" and "how to do it well" varity for all age levels, as well as the inculcation of values emphasizing the virtues of nonwork. But students who will have the most time free for leisure will be mostly from social backgrounds that are (so far, at least) little interested in the creative use of leisure and are made uncomfortable in the absence of the self-respect and preoccupation that derive from a job which takes up much of their time. These students are likely to be in the less experimental, less imaginative schools. Yet, in effect, the debate will be about just these schools. Even assuming that social pressures and the inclinations of school boards and parents favor such experiments, it is far from clear that teaching leisure-oriented values in school environments comprised of teachers, administrators, and plant-oriented toward operational efficiency and the production of workers is possible. While debate and experiments are very likely to increase, it is unlikely that by 1980 the formal educational system will be able to deal with leisure on the scale or with the emphasis that the topic deserves. (Other means that are likely to be evolved are discussed in the chapter on recreation.)

For all the reasons discussed above—the need for nation-wide occupational retraining and updating, the need to educate for more meaningful leisure hours, the economic necessity to keep unskilled young people out of the competitive labor force, earlier retirement, the increasing numbers of older adults seeking more education—it will gradually come to be recognized that, for either work or leisure, education can no longer be something essentially completed halfway through a person's third decade, at the latest. Erratically and unevenly during the next twenty years, we will experiment with and begin to establish a multilevel educational system which will encourage those of any age to continue their education for both work and leisure from wherever they left off to wherever their abilities permit them to go. (13) But we begin from a very low level and have a long way to go.

The most damning single fact about higher education today is that among nearly 2,500 accredited and unaccredited institutions there seem to be fewer than half a dozen radical experiments dedicated to testing new conceptions of what college life, and hence adult life, are capable of becoming. Unless not only the scholars and teachers and administrators who launch new ventures, but the parents and philanthropists who support them, all show more courage and imagination in the next decade than they have in the past, the fruits of universal higher education are likely to taste rather tinny. (14)

References

1. Carnegie Corporation of New York *Quarterly,* "Education and Politics," January 1963, Vol. XI, No. 1.

2. Mead, Margaret, "Problems of the Late Adolescent and Young Adult," *Golden Anniversary White House Conference on Children and Youth,* Department of Health, Education and Welfare. Washington, D.C.: U. S. Government Printing Office, 1960, p. 3.

3. Mechner, Francis, and Donald A. Cook, "Behavioral Technology and Manpower Development," New York: Basic Systems Incorporated, 1964.

4. Schramm, Wilbur, *Programed Instruction Today and Tomorrow.* New York: Fund for the Advancement of Education, 1962, pp. 37–38.

5. Jencks, Christopher, "Schoolmaster Rickover," *The New Republic,* Vol. 148, No. 9, Washington, D.C., March 2, 1963, p. 15.

6. Sanford, Nevitt, ed., *The American College: A Psychological and Social Interpretation of the Higher Learning.* New York: John Wiley & Sons, 1962, p. 17.

7. Hechinger, Fred M., "Education: A New Pattern—Colleges Face Dramatic Changes in Student Population," New York *Times,* September 16, 1962.

8. President's Committee on Youth Employment, *The Challenge of Jobless Youth.* Washington, D.C.: Government Printing Office, 1963.

9. Chase, Edward T., "Learning to Be Unemployable," *Harper's,* Vol. 226, No. 1355, April 1963, pp. 33–40.

10. Westervelt, Esther, *The Recruitment and Training of Education/Vocational Counselors of Girls and Women* (mimeo.), President's Commission on the Status of Women, Washington, D.C., March 14, 1963.

11. Friedenberg, Edgar Z., *The Vanishing Adolescent.* New York: Dell Publishing Co., New York, 1962.

12. Mead, Margaret, "Outdoor Recreation in the Context of Emerging American Cultural Values: Background Considerations," in *Trends in American Living and Outdoor Recreation,* Outdoor Recreation Resources Review Commission Study Report 22, Washington, D.C., 1962, p. 24.

13. Mead, Margaret, "Thinking Ahead: Why is Education Obsolete?" *Harvard Business Review,* Vol. 36, No. 6, p. 23.

14. Jencks, Christopher, "The Next Thirty Years in the Colleges," *Harper's,* October 1961, p. 128.

Supplementary References

Bailey, Stephen K., Richard T. Frost, Paul E. Marsh, and Robert C. Wood, *Schoolmen and Politics, A Study of State Aid to Education in the Northeast,* Vol. 1 of The Economics and Politics of Public Education. Syracuse, N.Y.: Syracuse University Press, 1962.

Bowles, Frank H., "Patterns of Dominance and Choice," *College Board Review,* No. 38, Spring 1959, pp. 5–10.

Bricks and Mortarboards—A Report on College Planning and Building, Educational Facilities Laboratories, Inc., New York: Ford Foundation, 1964.

Bruner, Jerome S., *The Process of Education.* Cambridge, Mass.: Harvard University Press, 1962.

"Education in the Age of Science," *Daedalus,* Gerald Holton, ed., American Academy of Arts and Sciences, Winter 1959.

David, Henry, ed., *Education and Manpower.* New York: Columbia University Press, 1960.

De Grazia, Alfred, ed., "The New Educational Technology," *The American Behavioral Scientist,* Vol. VI, No. 3, Trenton, N.J., November 1962.

Drucker, Peter, "Education in the New Technology," *Think,* Vol. 28, No. 6, June 1962, pp. 3–5.

Evans, Luther H., and George E. Arnstein, eds., *Automation and the Challenge to Education.* Washington, D.C.: National Education Association, 1962.

Jacobs, P. E., *Changing Values in College.* New York: Harper & Row, 1957.

Jencks, Christopher, "Slums and Schools," Parts I and II, *The New Republic,* Vol. 147, No. 10 and 11, September 10, 1962, pp. 19–22, and No. 12, September 17, 1962, pp. 13–16.

Kimball, Solon T., and James E. McClellan, *Education and the New America.* New York: Random House, Inc., 1962.

Martin, Roscoe C., *Government and the Suburban School,* Vol. 2 of The Economics and Politics of Public Education. Syracuse, N.Y.: Syracuse University Press, 1962.

Mayer, Martin, *The Schools.* New York: Harper & Row, 1961.

Munger, Frank J. and Richard R. Fenno, Jr., *National Politics and Federal Aid to Education,* Vol. 3 of The Economics and Politics of Public Education. Syracuse, N.Y.: Syracuse University Press, 1962.

Rivlin, Alice M., *The Role of the Federal Government in Financing Higher Education.* Washington, D.C.: The Brookings Institution, 1961.

Sexton, Patricia Cayo, *Education and Income: Inequalities in Our Public Schools.* New York: Viking Press, 1961.

Sufrin, Sidney C., *Issues in Federal Aid to Education,* Vol. 4 of The Economics and Politics of Public Education. Syracuse, N.Y.: Syracuse University Press, 1962.

Tannenbaum, Abraham J., *Adolescent Attitudes toward Academic Brilliance.* New York: Bureau of Publications, Teachers College, Columbia University, 1962.

Wrenn, C. Gilbert, *The Counselor in a Changing World.* Washington, D.C.: American Personnel and Guidance Association, 1962.

SECTION

The Consequences of
the Conditions·
Modes of Expression

CHAPTER

10

WORK

IT IS unclear now what skills will be needed where, when, and in what numbers during the years ahead. But it is clear that rapidly changing technologies will put increasing demands on society to anticipate these changes and to plan for them. Both the individual worker and the institutions responsible for his welfare will need the knowledge and the resources for meeting these changed demands in time to adjust to them and on sufficient scale to avoid serious social and economic disruptions.

PLANNING OCCUPATIONAL NEEDS

The combination of needs produced by our growing population *per se* and the expanding use of complicated social and technological machinery will increasingly require professionals of all kinds, supported by both highly trained and relatively unskilled technicians. Of course the shopkeeper, deliveryman, house painter, meter reader, sales clerk, tailor, and so on, will not disappear—certainly not during the next twenty years. Here, we will not attempt to speculate about the future of the conventional work force. Some such jobs will rapidly diminish, as have those of elevator operator and the coal miner; some may well increase. In this section will be speculations about the direction of those general occupational categories which will be of special or new importance in tomorrow's world and which, as such, offer new problems and opportunities for youth. Daniel Bell sees the trend this way:

To speak rashly: if the dominant figures of the past hundred and fifty years have been the entrepreneur, the businessman, and the executive, the "new men" are the research scientists, the mathematicians, the economists and the managers of the new computer technology; and the dominant institutions of the new society—in the sense of providing the most creative challenges and enlisting its best talents—will be the intellectual institutions. The leadership of the new society will not rest with the businessmen or the corporation as we know it (for production and most other elements of industry will have become routinized), but with the research corporations, the industrial laboratories, the experimental stations, and the universities. And the skeleton structure of that new society is already visible. (1)

Data or models about society adequate for predicting job needs are some years off, for the methodology and criteria for selecting valid predictive data in the face of high rates of technological change are still in their formulative stage. The difficulty of developing such models and using them will for some time be exacerbated by what Herbert E. Striner describes as:

. . . the tremendous fragmentation of organizational responsibility for dealing with increasing demands on society to anticipate changes in the types of work that will be needed. With this fragmentation of responsibility, there is an increasing problem of using information which we already have in order to deal with problems of technological unemployment and to begin to forecast new areas of employment. (2)

If and when such models are developed, the data will have to be collected regularly, nationally, and in great detail in order to anticipate specific job and professional needs for specific regions at specific future times. And they will have to be used with great wisdom if they are not to lead to inflexible planning.

Not all citizens will encourage such data collecting. This program probably would add to the tax burden, since the most likely operator of this costly and elaborate public-interest facility would be the government. In addition, a successful job-anticipating system will require an important modification of the free-enterprise system: valid information about job needs will reveal something about a company's long-term production and market plans, information conventionally guarded as part of the strategy of competition.

The resulting turmoil of divided control, conflicting values, and inadequate methods and data will mean that for many years occupational forecasting, and even the matching of available jobs with available unemployed, will be more or less makeshift and inadequate.

EFFECTS OF CYBERNATION

Although many new technologies will alter the job market, it is clear that, barring unforeseen developments, automation and computers will have the most important over-all consequences for the composition of the labor market. Present extrapolations of future job opportunities, based on yesterday's and today's world, will prove to be wrong in important ways. Cybernation has only begun to make its impact. Its effects on employment will be enormous. In the words of Walter Buckingham:

During the 1960's, it will be necessary to create an even greater number of job opportunities—perhaps as many as 4 million or more job opportunities every year—to provide employment for the average yearly growth in the labor force of 1,350,000 and the possible annual displacement of as many as 2.5 million or more workers from rising productivity.(3)

In the next ten to twenty years cybernation will disrupt the whole labor market, from executives to menials. In addition to the unskilled, many blue-collar workers, engineers, and middle-level engineers and managers presently doing skilled work will find their jobs usurped by cybernation. For many it will be an anxious period indeed; for others a most exciting and rewarding one. (4, 5) Undoubtedly, cybernation will be accelerated as national and international competition increase, as industry uses the 7 per cent investment credit especially designed to help defray costs of more efficient machinery (passed in 1962), as minimum wage increases and demands for shorter work hours make it more attractive to replace the unskilled with machines. Since cybernation usually means change in the whole production, distribution, and control system rather than just parts of it, ingenious methods and detailed data will be needed to estimate where, when, and how many jobs will be available for those with specific educational prerequisites. As Buckingham says: "On the average every electronic computer puts 35 people out of work and changes the kind of work for 105 additional workers. Since the United States alone is producing over 10,000 computers per year, this multiplies out to 350,000 jobs disappearing every year and another 1,050,000 that will require retraining."(6) Cybernated systems are more efficient if they work continuously. There are already indications of a trend toward 24-hour operations; organizations that process much paper work as the basis for the next day's decisions and actions are beginning to run their data processing at night.(7) We should see, over the years ahead, an increasing portion of both white-collar and blue-collar personnel working on other than the present conventional schedule. If this trend becomes general enough, servicing activities will also find it worth while to remain open 24 hours. Thus, we probably are beginning to move into a world which, much more than in the past, will work and play around the clock.

ATTITUDES TOWARD WORK ENVIRONMENT

As occupational training begins earlier and specialization becomes more frequently a prerequisite for secure, well-paying salaries, there will be increasing pressure on youth to make occupational choices in terms of objective talent or social need rather than subjective preference. Nevertheless, for some years at least, a large proportion of youth will continue to choose occupations that do not require very intensive preparation and which conform to conventional job expectations and aspirations. The result will be shortages in occupations requiring skills, commitment, and devoted preparation.

Except among some professionals there will be a growing awareness that one may change his type of job two or three times in a working career. Traditional expectations about settling down into a lifetime job, or at least doing the same thing all of one's working life subject to certain types of specified advancement, will give way more and more to a belief that what one does and when one changes jobs will depend on a rapidly changing technology over which the individual has little or no control. Among the skilled this state of what Eric Larrabee calls "permanent unpredictability" may be coped with by a deepening commitment to profession or skill rather than to job. Among some of the unskilled, the expectation that government will look after them if they are disemployed will encourage an indifference toward the organization worked for and little, if any, commitment to a particular task. The prevalence of sloppy work and indifferent workers is already all too evident; it will become more so as incentives to be precise decrease and where the work situation permits.

But a countertrend may also develop. Service businesses may try to compete by offering better service. They may, therefore, set higher standards of competence and deportment, and unions may very well support these as a means for limiting the number of people competing for union-controlled jobs. Also, those with better deportment and commitment may be more likely to be selected for the available jobs, especially if there is a large labor pool to choose from. However, it may well be that most of the people serviced will themselves not demand or appreciate better service, since they themselves lack such standards. It may also be that so few of those competing for jobs will possess the higher standards that there will not be enough candidates to provide a significant base for competition. And it may be that the management responsible for large service organizations will not find it economically worth while to cope with the operational problems raised by trying to offer distinctively better service. All in all, excellence and commitment probably will continue to be at least as scarce as they have always been in family, school, mass media, and mass service organizations.

THE PROFESSIONAL'S WORK
ENVIRONMENT

Over the next twenty years first-rate professionals will in most cases be in such short supply that for them a 60- to 70-hour work week will be closer to the norm than 40. This group will certainly tend toward a much longer work week than that required of most supporting technicians or unskilled workers (though some skilled technicians will be in short supply too and will also work long hours). It will take many years to provide the teachers, institutional changes, financing, and motivation in students and parents to increase the supply to meet the rapidly growing demand for top professionals. There are many different estimates of what the demand and supply will be in later years, and all of them suffer from the limitations discussed at the beginning of this chapter. (8) But, it is quite clear that those now over ten years old will not be trained as top professionals in such numbers as to provide an oversupply in most fields. Many of those who are infants now will face a more stimulating learning environment by 1970, but they will not move into the professional and skilled technical pool until after the 1980's. Then, too, the more extensive the learning, the later people will enter the job market.

Professionals will have to be very well trained in the fundamentals of their field, as well as in related matters. They will need to aspire to high work standards and, while the basic professions will not become obsolete, keeping on top of a profession will require a lifetime of acquiring new knowledge. With appropriate training in fundamentals and with minds which have not through disuse lost their ability to learn, these people will look forward to one career or another which directly evolves from their earlier training.

SCIENCE AND ENGINEERING

The demand for scientists and engineers will almost certainly be great for a long time to come (though substantial reductions in the present level of spending for defense research and development will very likely result in lower salaries and some temporary unemployment for many). Given the special role of scientists and engineers in tomorrow's world, it is worth speculating on plausible trends in occupational characteristics. The role and style of research and development engineering and of science will change over the next two decades. Government, industry, and the universities will increasingly become dependent on the presence and productivity of scientists and engineers. In the process these professions will become a powerful political lobby for money, policies, and programs of special benefit to scientists and engineers. Often backing them will be the institutions, agencies, and businesses which stand to gain from the exploitation of science and engineering.

As science becomes more recognized as a well-paid avenue to power and influence it will become more attractive to young people who aspire to power or who enjoy competition. Its popular image, even now changing, will shift from one stressing quiet, individual contemplation to one of aggressive, competitive, sociable action. This is not to say there will be no quiet contemplators, immune to the glamour and pay of "political" and "big" science—or, for that matter, that all scientists were so immune in the past. However, to a much greater extent than now, two types of scientist will be produced

and the explicit intentions of those using scientists and
the aspirations of those choosing careers as scientists
will be quite different, depending on the type chosen.

In addition to the increase in competitive, status-seek-
ing, power-wielding scientists and engineers, a smatter-
ing of science will be much more frequently a prerequisite for advancement in other careers. Science or
engineering will more often than not be recognized as a
means to some other career, as well as a career in itself.
In our society a lawyer's education has been a special
means for entry into many high-status jobs which of
themselves do not require a technical background in
law (in the USSR engineering has been the means of
entry). The many reasons for this include the importance of the law in guiding fortunes and business. For
analogous reasons, backgrounds that have included science will in the next two decades often be the most direct means for entering jobs of high status which of
themselves will not require a detailed knowledge of science. This will be true in the smaller organizations as
well as in the larger ones.

Not all scientists and engineers will need to be first-
rate minds intensely dedicated to their professions. This
is already the case and will become more so as more of
them fill managerial roles and do routine, directed, research and development tasks especially on the big research and development projects which industry, government, and nonprofit institutions will increasingly sponsor.
There will be many more opportunities for the mediocre
scientist and engineer, the "gentlemen scientists" as they
already have been called, who work a well-paid, modest
number of hours in pleasant surroundings at interesting
but not all-consuming tasks. Thus, there will develop the
realization that one can be a scientist or engineer without

being a "brain," much as there is recognition that to be a doctor or lawyer does not require the consummate talents or absolute dedication of the best in these professions. More young people will be attracted to science and engineering thereby. For these reasons, there will be much science and engineering done within those prevailing national values which do not take too seriously commitment, integrity, and brilliance. (9) However, there will be drastically fewer opportunities for engineers (and those in related occupations, such as draftsmen) whose competencies are limited to routine design tasks. Increasingly, these tasks will be done by computers.

Computers have developed designs that range from airplanes to architecture, from electrical circuits to clothing, from ship hulls to highways. The results have exhibited the constraints of an experienced human designer's feel for form and aesthetics and his canny knowledge of the possibilities and limitations of production facilities.
. . . The human designer, as the modifier of an automatic system, will work on improving system information . . . rather than solving the specific design problem being processed. Designers will design the designing system which designs the actual objects. (10)

MANAGEMENT

While many other professional activities will change their preoccupations, especially as they make more use of the computer to process data and simulate events, it is worth speculating about changes in the nature of management given the central and growingly professionalized role it will fill in rationalized organizations.

As indicated earlier, there will be special opportunities in management for those who have taken a minimum of science courses designed for businessmen, industrialists, or managers, courses that will not be beyond their abilities or jeopardize their chances to succeed in other studies needed for essentially nonscientific careers. Although the prerequisite of exposure to science will, to an extent, be ritualistic, it will be true that the first-rate executive or junior candidate for such a role will have to be familiar and comfortable with cybernetics, operations research, and the other techniques and technologies for organizational rationalization. More and more, the organizations that survive and grow in the world of the next two decades will be those which can use these techniques boldly and intelligently. The changeover in top management will not be sudden, but the trend is inevitable.

The relative number of career opportunities for middle management very likely will decrease, especially in large organizations. Supervisory tasks will disappear as the workers do. The routine "decision-making" activities which now occupy much of middle management will be taken over by computers, and decisions will be more centralized within top management. Top management will have much greater knowledge about and control over its organization as a result of the rationalization of middle-management activities and of computer-based information prepared especially for top decision making. (11)

The role of the truly creative top executive will become more difficult. Professor Raymond Bauer, of the Harvard Business School, suggests that:

. . . the demands on top management will probably be to deal with the outputs of technicians and computers, i.e., he will have to make value judgments and intuitive decisions within precisely defined parameters. This means that his job will be like it is now, but it will be much tougher because he will no longer be able to fudge issues. (12)

ARTISTS

If the economy remains reasonably prosperous, artists will be increasingly in demand and a greater proportion of them will be reasonably well paid, even for mediocre abilities. They will perform more and they will teach growing numbers of would-be amateur performers. The steady and sometimes spectacular growth in the proportion of those showing an interest in music, painting, and the other arts (often because the numbers have been so small to start with), suggests that increased numbers of potential amateurs, better education, and more time and money to spend on new experiences will provide ever bigger commercial markets for the arts and growing aesthetic appreciation for the artist. This new climate of recognition and awareness will open ancillary opportunities as well—as hobby consultants, guides on international tours, and so on.

The serious artist or student whose work is not popular or who is uninterested in being part of the art world just described will probably live and work much as he does now, with three exceptions. (a) He will be more likely to find an isolated social colony which will be congenial for him. (b) He will be more likely to find a patron, for as the popularity of art increases the opportunities for gaining status by supporting art—even an antisocial artist or one whose work is not popular—will increase. Such an artist will be "interesting" by virtue of his nonacceptance. (c) He will have a harder time maintaining his "separateness." The voracious novelty hunters—the mass media—will transfuse his very separateness into the society as they have done with beatniks, folk singers, and others, transforming their personal protests against "the system" into fads and fashions.

TECHNICIANS

The technician will sometimes be a skilled associate and aide of the professional, or he may be a skilled service man or woman such as an electrician, plumber, or hair stylist.

The poverty program, Peace Corps, and civil rights movement presage increasing opportunities for subprofessionals in social service activities where no machine can replace face-to-face human exchange. Professionals, overwhelmed with tasks a sensitive, intelligent technician could do, will surrender them to the right kinds of people rightly trained. The status and education for these people is presently unclear, but a recognized need for them will steadily increase. (13)

Human abstractors will be in growing demand for some years to come. Information will accumulate in unprecedented amounts as computers take over and as the number of human "information generators" increases. We will be faced with a data glut which threatens to make most newly discovered information almost useless: those who could use it will not know it exists. While automatic abstracting will increase substantially, during the next decade the demands for many types of abstracted information, especially qualitative knowledge and ideas, will exceed the capabilities of commercially available computers. It will be at the very least ten years before there will be an automatic capability reasonably adequate for abstracting nonscientific as well as scientific information which could benefit society. Therefore, human abstractors will be in growing demand for some years to come.

People with the special competencies will be needed to chair interdisciplinary work conferences. The interdisciplinary work session will increasingly be used as an

efficient and unique means for the exchange, enlargement, and application of knowledge. But the success and
efficiency of this form of data abstraction and data reduction depend on the art of chairmanship and work-
group organizing. Those who combine the scarce talents
of trained interpersonal sensitivity and a generalized
capacity to guide technical discourse will be in great demand.

There will be a related need for more science writers
to interpret science to the laymen, to interpret one specialist to another, and to help scientists write papers
clearly enough in the first place so they can be efficiently and accurately abstracted. (Even with these improvements there is no reason to believe that enough
people will be capable of dealing adequately with the
increasing data glut. Much that would be useful will be
lost or delayed in application.)

For many at the technician-level, working hours will
be fewer, probably around 35 hours per week, possibly
by early in the 1970's. However, to the extent their services are crucial and in scarce supply, some may work
as long hours as the top professionals they support.
Their work will be relatively highly specialized: as technology changes, so, too, will the numbers of people and
type of training needed to fill the job opportunities.
There will then be a growing requirement for well-
trained technicians who will also have the social and
intellectual prerequisites for effective learning and relearning. As cybernation enlarges the geography of industry and commerce, and as the megalopolis evolves
from the city, the technician and the unskilled worker
will have to become as physically mobile as are many
professionals and managers. New jobs will, as likely as
not, be in another part of the country or in another coun-

try and the technician will expect to move to where his
retrained abilities can be used.

Blue-collar jobs, such as construction work and truck
driving, will survive. However, over the next two decades many such jobs will disappear or be transformed
as fabrication, manufacturing, and distribution methods change. Some will be refined as more skill is required; some will be downgraded. (For example, the
construction industry probably will begin to change substantially in the next decade or so, as automatically prefabricated substructures become more commonplace
and as radical construction techniques are used to meet
the housing and working needs of a larger population
and to overcome the increasing expense of conventional
building methods.)

THE UNSKILLED

Contrary to popular belief, cybernation does not presage
the end of dull jobs: automatic machinery does not
necessarily mean the upgrading of any job which sur-
vives. Tending a complex of automatic machinery need
not require great skill. There will be many menial technician jobs, as well as more interesting ones now popularly thought to be inevitable concomitants of cybernation. (14)

Office jobs, especially routine and unskilled clerical
ones, will be increasingly replaced by cybernated equipment. As the population grows and, with it, paper work
of all sorts, the efficiency of cybernation will make its
use more and more attractive. Even small organizations
will be able to replace much of their clerical staff by
renting time and memory capacity in computer facilities established to service many small organizations

through data transmission via telephone and teletype.

It is not generally appreciated that cybernating data processing in an office usually only *begins* by using machines to replace people doing routine, discrete data-processing tasks. It then becomes worth while to reorganize forms and procedures so that more and more of the total flow of office activity can be handled directly by the machines. Already, the mail into some organizations contains forms prepunched or so marked that computers can deal directly with the information and requests on the forms, carrying the process through by establishing the permanent records, analyzing trends, altering inventories, establishing production schedules, and so on. Thus many activities are reorganized—including relations with the outside world—so that the *whole* system can be more effectively rationalized.

In 1963, the Labor Department estimated that a third of the female work force was "clerical": this represented about 70 per cent of all clerical workers. Women now are about a third of the total work force and are expected to remain that proportion into the 1970's. Since, in 1970, about 28 per cent of the fourteen- to nineteen-year-olds and 45 per cent of the twenty- to twenty-four-year-old women are expected to be available for work, serious economic, human, and retraining problems are very likely to arise in the absence of sufficient advanced training for more-needed skills in high school. (15)

It is plausible that, between them, unskilled women and well-to-do women might resurrect the occupation of live servant. In addition to providing employment for the unskilled, such an occupation would allow more skilled women, who are more likely than not to be married to well-to-do husbands, some time to use these

skills away from home. Whether the job of private servant could be made self-fulfilling for both parties remains
to be seen. (It might not be impossible. For example,
the government might endow the job with patriotic virtue
because it contributed doubly to the economic growth of
the nation!)

Over the next two decades there will continue to be
many unskilled jobs which cannot be cybernated, or for
which it is not economically feasible to do so, or which
become menial by being cybernated. But if the size of
the unemployed unskilled labor force increases, those
unskilled jobs for which good wages can be paid on the
basis of labor scarcity will steadily decline. Unless a way
can be found to make them pay well or to give the
worker some sense of self-respect, performance will seriously deteriorate through insufficient motivation to do a
good job.

During the next decade at least, high numbers of
school dropouts, unskilled women returning to the work
force, blue-collar and white-collar workers with insufficient training in how to learn and relearn, and slum and
rural adolescents with similar limitations, as well as the
hard core of functionally disemployed victims of illiter-
acy and physical, emotional, and mental inadequacies
—all will provide too large a reservoir of competitors
for the remaining menial tasks. The necessary research
and pilot studies to develop means (if they exist at all)
for overcoming some sorts of deficiencies *en masse*
will not soon be developed. The economic and ethical
problems involved in coping with this problem on the
scale needed will be enormous. One example: as it
becomes clearer that job accessibility is increasingly
dependent on physical mobility, more arrangements will
evolve to provide the economic and psychological sup-

port necessary to encourage the unskilled or little-skilled to go where jobs are available. At the very least, this will mean an extended social welfare program transcending the different state residence requirements, and a mortgage guarantee program which will make it possible for people with low income to move, even if their house is unsold. Since the supply of unskilled will often exceed the demand, there probably will be little incentive for states or businesses to pay these costs directly. Federal support would seem to be the most plausible trend, but not a rapid one; to many taxpayers and politicians it will appear easier to leave the poor and politically impotent where they are than to undertake the elaborate, expensive, and politically delicate programs needed to give them the ability to move. The political issues and human problems will involve many extra-economic considerations, as, for example, what will be the basis of choosing which unskilled can move to what jobs where?

If, as seems likely, the social and economic problems of this large group reach the point where they threaten the nation's welfare, the government will at the very least enlarge legislation and public works programs to encourage the employment of the untrained. Extensive public works programs are most probable, since only these will make use of large numbers of untrained workers who also lack the motives or abilities for retraining. But it should be noted that such programs, in the absence of any long-term and extensive effort to eliminate the *sources* of low capability, will simply prolong the existence of a group ever less capable of taking a productive place in an ever more complex and sophisticated world.

To help avoid such occupational inadequacies and to

reduce the number of competing low-skilled workers, the government is very likely, sooner or later, to introduce programs to keep adolescents out of the competitive work force. Legislation prohibiting adolescent workers, except under special economic conditions, will be one means. Paid opportunities to learn skills outside the formal school context and grants contingent on remaining in school are other alternatives. This, however, will be a touchy problem. Teachers will be overworked, especially in the underprivileged schools where adolescents might be staying only because they are paid to. The counterproductive consequences are obvious. If this sort of program is successful at all it will probably be available only for students who do have the ability and ambition to do well. Clearly, administering such a program would have its political difficulties.

Similarly, older unskilled workers will be increasingly excluded from the work force, probably through payment of direct subsidies from government, industry, and unions, and by paying them to go to special schools for leisure-time skill training.

WOMEN AT WORK

Obviously, the proportion of unskilled women is far larger than the corresponding proportion of men. The reasons are many, not the least of which is that many college-educated women have preferred to opt for marriage and children, with a job in the interim, and have been educated to viewpoints and ways that make it difficult to alter this option after child-raising is finished. (16) Increasing emphasis on the skill shortage and on opportunities for women, increasing opportunities for women to refresh or enlarge a skill acquired before child-raising, increasing opportunities to work part time while child-raising, will gradually change this pattern. However, unless there is an all-out effort to change the whole educational and retraining context for women, the process will be slow. Several factors militate against rapid revision.

In the first place, the ambiguous and ambivalent attitudes and expectations of female youth, in part derived from and supported by their mothers *and* fathers, will be hard to change quickly, because it is hard to change parents' perspectives quickly. (17)

In the second place, because there are now so few professionally and technically trained women, and because of traditional perspectives and male prejudices, it will be difficult to enlarge rapidly the female membership in faculties of schools stressing the professions and other technical careers. Without female teachers as models, women will be less likely to move rapidly into the work force. While there will be increases in professionally and technically trained women, they will represent only a relatively small part of the female work force in the next two decades and they will tend to have jobs customarily defined as especially appropriate for women. (18)

In the third place, while there is much talk about encouraging women to take a more active role, male-oriented and male-dominated institutions are not likely to change attitudes rapidly enough to absorb a highly competent female professional and technological work force at a rate great enough to demonstrate to women, espeially to those surveying the adult scene from their college perspectives, that it is worth aspiring to professional and technical roles. Although steps have been taken to improve the situation, it is significant that as of October 1962, with all the talk in government over the years about the need for female talent, it was reported that:

In the professional ranks [of the Federal Government], 40,000 or 18 percent, are women. But 20,000 of these are nurses. The median salary of men holding professional jobs is four grades higher than that of women. In the more than 2,000 supergrades, at GS-16, 17, and 18, there are just 24 women . . . 76.8 percent of *all* women employees are in the lowest five grades of the General Schedule. (19)

In the fourth place, although there will be (in principle, if not in fact) plenty of room at the top for women of superior mind and training, whether or not there will be places for the women of middling talent and training is not nearly so evident. At this level of ability men will be threatened with disemployment, whether they be middle managers, mediocre maintenance men, or computer programers. So long as conventional views of man as the breadwinner prevail, jobs for mediocre people and retraining for better jobs, when they are available, are more likely to go to needy men than to women. And this conventional view is not likely to change very much, in the United States at least, during the coming decade.

However, it is also perfectly clear that the need for women with middle-level skills will be enormously great in areas that are presently defined as appropriate for women: primary and secondary school teachers, recreation leaders, administrators, managers and operators of service activities, trained aides and assistants to every kind of highly skilled professional, technicians of all kinds, and so on. The growing trend for older skilled and semiskilled women to want to move back into the labor market—or at least out of the house—indicates a potentially vast source of both highly skilled and trainable labor. It is not at all clear, however, that we will develop quickly the resources to exploit this invaluable labor pool. Imagination on a wide scale; a willingness on the part of institutions to change their conventional regulations so they can use this capability even when it lacks some of the traditional prerequisites for membership; the establishment of large-scale training and retraining programs—all present problems as formidable as those raised by the efficient use of male labor. We have yet to attack the work problems of men on the scale required, and they are not hindered by views about "woman's place."

NEGROES

The *numbers* of skilled Negroes will increase, as will the opportunities to acquire skills and to use them. This will be due to their growing political power, better organization of pressure groups, and to changed attitudes on the part of many whites. If an enfeebled economy or disemployment do not lead to desperate competition for jobs requiring those skills with which Negroes are now making their way for the first time, their accomplishments should make it progressively easier for more Negroes to be accepted and for more to be motivated to seek training for skilled jobs.

But the gap between the *proportions* of white and Negro skilled labor will increase, too, at least over the next decade, for there will continue to be much prejudice in the white community, and large portions of the Negro population will continue to have inadequate standards of performance and motivation. There is no reason to believe that our institutions will change so radically and swiftly in the next few years as to provide, in David

Riesman's phrase, the "better than equal" resources in living conditions, education, training, and job opportunities needed to convince the large majority of underprivileged Negroes that middle-class opportunities and acceptability as the social equals of whites can be attained and, therefore, are worth striving for. But unless such extraordinary resources are made available, a large majority of Negroes will lose out in the competition for superior jobs because of inadequate values and inadequate education, even in the presence of such values. Without such changes in national effort, the overall national trend will be in the direction of a white, privileged, skilled, intellectual-professional society and a Negro menial, unskilled, worker society. This inequality in the skilled work force will, in all likelihood, have its inverse at the unskilled end; in too many cases Negro workers will continue to be fired before whites. Indeed, we may well face acute crises in the next few years. Unless very well-planned and wide-ranging efforts are carried through, the Negro seeking a job for which he has been recently trained will find it unavailable—cybernated out of existence or taken by a white, who has also been displaced, perhaps from an even more skilled job, by technological change.

References

1. Bell, Daniel, "The Post-Industrial Society," Liberty Mutual Insurance Company Forum, Boston, June 14, 1962.

2. Private correspondence.

3. Buckingham, Walter, "The Great Employment Controversy," *The Annals,* "Automation," Charles C. Killingsworth, special editor, Vol. 340, American Academy of Political and Social Science, Philadelphia, March 1962, pp. 46–52.

4. Mann, Floyd C., "Psychological and Organizational Impacts," in John T. Dunlop, ed., *Automation and Technological Change,* (The American Assembly Columbia University Series). Englewood Cliffs, N.J.: Prentice-Hall, Inc., 1962, pp. 43–65.

5. Glazer, William, "Automation and Joblessness, *Atlantic Monthly,* Vol. 210, August 1962, pp. 43–47.

6. Buckingham, Walter, "Automation's Impact on Skills and Employment," Voice of America Program Services, Automation Series, U. S. Information Agency, Washington, January 8 and 11, 1963.

7. Hoos, Ida R., "Automation in the Office," Voice of America Central Program Services, Automation Series, U. S. Information Agency, Washington, 1962.

8. McBee, Susanna, "Education Not Meeting Job Needs," Washington *Post,* April 21, 1963, p. E–1.

9. Storer, Norman, "The Coming Changes in American Science," *Science,* Vol. 142, October 25, 1963, pp. 464–467.

10. Börje Langefors, "Automated Design: More of It Can Be Done on an Automatic Computer Than Most Designers Are Willing to Admit," *International Science and Technology,* February 1964, pp. 90 and 91.

11. Leavitt, Harold J. and Thomas L. Whistler, "Management in the 1980's," *Harvard Business Review,* Vol. 36, No. 6, November–December 1958, p. 41.

12. Private correspondence.

13. Pines, Maya, "Training Housewives as Psychotherapists," *Harper's,* Vol. 224, No. 1343, National Institute of Mental Health April 1962, pp. 37–42. Rioch, M.J., et al., "NIMH Pilot Study in Training Mental Health Counselors," *American Journal of Orthopsychiatry,* Vol. 33, No. 4, July 1963, pp. 678–689.

14. Bright, James R., "Does Automation Raise Skill Requirements?," *Harvard Business Review,* Vol. 36, No. 4, July–August 1958, pp. 85–98.

15. U. S. Department of Labor, *Manpower Challenge of the 1960's.* Washington, D.C.: U. S. Government Printing Office, 1961, p. 7.

16. Cassara, Beverly Benner, ed., *American Women: The Changing Image.* Boston: Beacon Press, 1962.

17. Bettleheim, Bruno, "Growing Up Female," *Harper's* (Special Supplement), Vol. 225, No. 1349, October 1962, pp. 120–128.

18. Riesman, David, "Permissiveness and Sex Roles," *Marriage and Family Living,* Vol. 21, August 1959, pp. 211–217.

19. Harrison, Evelyn, "The Quiet Revolution," *Civil Service Journal,* Vol. 3, No. 2, October–December 1962, pp. 7, 24.

Supplementary References

Feldman, Lloyd, and Michael R. Peevey, *Young Workers: Their Special Training Needs* (Manpower Research Bulletin No. 3). Washington, D.C.: U. S. Department of Labor, 1963.

O'Toole, Thomas, "White Collar Automation," *The Reporter,* December 5, 1963, pp. 24–27.

Seligman, Ben B., "Man, Work & The Automated Feast," *Commentary,* Vol. 34, July 1962, pp. 9–19.

Social Dynamite, The Report of the Conference on Unemployed, Out-of-School Youth in Urban Areas, National Committee for Children and Youth, Inc., Washington, D.C., 1961.

U. S. Department of Labor, *Manpower Report of the President and a Report on Manpower Requirements, Resources, Utilization, and Training.* Washington, D.C.: U. S. Government Printing Office, March 1963.

Weiss, Robert S., and David Riesman, "Social Problems and Disorganization in the World of Work," in Robert E. Merton and Robert A. Nisbet, eds., *Contemporary Social Problems.* New York: Harcourt, Brace & World, Inc., 1961, pp. 459–514.

Wilensky, Harold L. "Work, Careers, and Social Integration," *International Social Science Journal,* Vol. XII, UNESCO, Paris, Fall 1960, pp. 543–560.

Wirtz, W. Willard, *On Research and Training Activities under the Manpower Development and Training Act.* Washington, D.C.: U. S. Government Printing Office (Transmitted to the Congress), February 1963.

CHAPTER

11

LEISURE

IN THE next two decades recreation and other nonwork activities will be increasingly important in the United States. For those with good incomes, other than first-rate professionals, working days or weeks will be shorter or vacations will be longer. The well paid will have more spending money and more encouragement to consume. Leisure activities will provide an outlet from rationalized work environments and will offer to some people release from the frustration and anxieties of the general world situation. "Leisure" will also be a growing problem for the slum-ridden, the poorly paid menial worker, the unemployed and the disemployed of all ages—and for those concerned with their welfare.

During at least the next ten years substantial changes in present values and behavior about work and leisure are most unlikely, especially if one's occupational future looks precarious. These values and behaviors vary somewhat but, generally speaking, those who will have the most free time (as distinct from unemployment-caused idle time) will be people who are uncomfortable if they are not "doing something"; who need to keep busy or to

be distracted; who need to feel that pleasure derived
from leisure is a reward for work done or is quasi-medi-
cally justified by being "good for you." (1, 2) Consequently, not all who have the time and money will be
comfortable with their additional leisure or able to use
it productively. Many will use increases in free time for
second jobs (which could become illegal if unemployment becomes more serious). Many others will anx-
iously "keep busy" or withdraw into endless passive
spectatorship.

By the 1980's, perhaps, some changes in attitude toward and use of leisure may begin to be noticeable. The
insufficiency of the conventional uses of leisure; the in-
controvertible evidences that working time will continue
to decrease; the growing emphasis on lifetime learning
and relearning; and the general emphasis on the mind-
oriented worker society will make the virtue and
purposes of leisure an important topic for leadership attention, program planning, and implementation. The beginnings of this trend, of course, already exist in certain
organizations and in more frequent public expressions
of concern. (3)

WHO WILL HAVE MORE TIME?

During the next two decades most first-rate professionals
will continue to work around 60 hours a week. Youth,
at least those planning professional careers, will have
substantially less leisure time than they now do as
school hours increase and vacation time decreases.
(Hours probably will not increase very much for the
nonprofessionally oriented student. If they do increase,
they may be devoted to less difficult topics—indeed, to
topics related to the cultivation of free time—and herein

may lie one more factor discouraging professional ambitions.) Those with the most hours and money to spend in leisure will fall between overworked "social servants" and the underpaid underskilled.

Increasing home cybernation, prepackaged household services, longer school hours for children, more community nurseries, younger grandparents, cheaper and sometimes faster intercity transportation, and possibly servants, all should begin to alleviate the load of household tasks which now overburden the housewife and mother. Obviously, the free time gleaned from these circumstances will belong to families with good incomes. Sufficient hours should be freed by this combination of factors to allow the reasonably well-off woman to play a much larger role than she does today in establishing the directions and styles of leisure activities.

Some women whose attitudes about work differ from those of men, and some who possess the image or role of teacher, social worker, civic projects leader, and so on, will have had most experience with recreation and leisure and will be in a position to contribute most to the transformation of values about recreation and leisure (when it begins to be clearer to men that the issue is a major one).

FORMS OF LEISURE

Travel, especially international travel, will be ever more popular with those who can afford it, if the military-political state of the world encourages it. Opportunities for low-cost chartered air transportation will increase; costs of ship travel will decrease as hydrofoils are used more extensively and as more people find that the need for fast transportation is reduced as vacation time is increased.

As a result of expanding population and expanding urban areas, plus lagging or nonexistent programs to set aside recreation areas for future use, close-in recreation areas will grow more crowded and the time needed to reach more remote areas will increase. Facilities used by a few people at a time will be saturated even if the wait is long, because there will be enough people to saturate them who are willing to wait. Waiting itself will be a way to fill free time. Commuting for hours, waiting around the clubhouse, first tee, ski lift, or boat landing will be the natural evolution of standing around the street corner or sitting around the drugstore. Indeed, sufficient exposure to "just waiting" may unwittingly build habits which later can be applied to the cultivation of less active, more "loafing" leisure.

By the 1970's it is plausible that the economic need to share jobs (but to do so efficiently), the number of people at all levels being re-educated or updated at any given time, and the growing tendency toward around-the-clock operations of all sorts may well have led to a general trend of longer vacations with little diminution in the hours worked per week. If so, at any given time substantial portions of the population will be on extensive vacations or sabbaticals. This would make feasible intensive use of far-away recreation areas. If this should come about, the opportunities for participation in activities used by a few people at a time would increase greatly, if the recreation areas were developed. There will not be enough such areas in the next several years; however, social pressures and economic opportunities will encourage considerable expansion, especially later, by both government and private enterprise. Indeed, recreation is likely to become a far larger industry than it now is. (4) It will be a source of jobs for some of the unskilled and underendowed; there will be lots of beds to make, meals to serve, flowers to water, walls to paint (if they're not plastic). Recreation services are likely to replace crops on many small and economically marginal farms.

The trend to active sports and related activities will continue, but as the load on available outlets becomes heavier and heavier not all those who would like direct participation in low-density recreation will be willing to fight traffic, commute for hours, or make reservations days or weeks in advance. Even if they were willing to, many simply would not be able to find congenial circumstances. Some portion, then, will at least partially abdicate direct participation for vicarious involvement in high-density spectator sports and other recreations. Facilities for high-density, vicarious participation and spectatorship will increase greatly in the years ahead. Professional and amateur sporting events, theatricals, concerts, and circuses of all sorts will proliferate, as will museum touring and similar activities. But television, in particular, will further increase its appeal as the key to vicarious living.

In time, there will be more television programs emphasizing culture and education. The size of the audience will increase, fed especially by the large younger generation and, to a smaller extent, by those retiring earlier who enjoy such offerings but who could not devote as much time to them when they were working. Women returning to or finding themselves interested in professional or semiprofessional activities once they are freed of child-raising will also swell the audience. Indeed, while they *are* child-raising, such programs will help them to prepare for eventual jobs. All in all, an audience supporting a very substantial educational and cultural TV output will grow. These programs may be supported through subscriptions, or may be sponsored by commercial groups because the audience will be large enough to provide good markets for appropriate sponsors.

Government and foundation support for cultural and educational TV will expand to provide more money, films, and other resources in order to meet the recreational and intellectual needs of an ever more complex society. Business and unions are likely to contribute as well, partially to try to improve their public images (especially if technology-based job losses seriously affect whatever favorable attitudes there are toward unions, business, and industry); partially out of a sense of *noblesse oblige* (much as firms now commission famous architects to build their offices and laboratories); and partially because of an appreciation that this society will need more education and culture and more experiments with substance and format than the formal educational system will provide during this period.

There is no indication that the quality of most commercial TV and radio will change much, at least during the next decade. Since the values of most of those watching and originating it will not change markedly, neither will commercial TV, especially given the economics of network competition and the growth of specialized channels and support for cultural and educational TV. (5)

Seeking sensation and novelty *per se* will increasingly be attractive recreational and leisure-time goals for that substantial portion of the population which will have the time and money for leisure but not the inclination to cultivate it in other ways. These activities require no special training to enjoy beyond the ability to find and pay for them. The former prerequisite will be amply supplied by advertising and the cornucopia of attractive "things" will be endlessly diverting.

New electronic and solid-state physics developments, as well as new materials and fabricating methods, will result in an immense variety of gadgets, as well as more substantial devices, to temporarily titillate the purchaser, occasionally through the very mystery of the nature of their operation. Most of these popular novelties will be about as contributive to a significantly better life and as meaningful for the direction and function of society as today's motor-driven pepper mill or battery-powered highball stirrer and tomorrow's toaster that butters the toast, or wall TV. But discovering these novelties and possessing them will reward those who believe in the virtues of consumption and who find the larger world progressively more difficult to make part of themselves —and such consumption will, of course, help sustain the economy.

Growing population, cheaper production, and distribution via automation will result in the steady proliferation of special-interest books, magazines, radio programs, and newspapers. Special-interest magazines of very high quality will be published in greater variety, over the next twenty years, as the better educated younger groups become consumers. However, much of what is produced will be rather thin stuff, since only a small portion of any interest group will pursue its interest deeply, and because, as with many functionally equivalent products produced by many competitors, much of the material can be only marginally differentiated.

A large portion of the mass media will continue to sensationalize the world's happenings, providing entertainment and diversion under the guise of news. The already extensive tendency to use public relations hand-outs from government, business, and private organizations as if they were the products of news reporting will continue and competition for attention in event-packed papers will encourage more and more sensational press-news releases. Lack of sufficient good reporters to cope with the day-to-day world and local issues will exacerbate this situation. Those interested in details will look to high-quality magazine reporting and syndicated columnists and use the newspapers chiefly for the broad picture, local news, and shopping information. (6)

The most radical opportunity for new sensations at the personal level will be through the use of chemicals which affect perceptions of self and the environment, by intensifying or modifying sensations and emotions. Made safe, non-habit-forming, and cheap—all of which seems well within the realm of possibility—they may provide by far the most intense exposure to new experience available. (7) If they do indeed broaden and sharpen the sense of self and the larger universe, the results could be all to the good. If they discourage participation in the humdrum of organized complexity, they will be a threat to the operation of society. In this case, use of the chemicals will no doubt be illegal or, more likely, available only to people meeting certain standards of conduct and need. If use is restricted, they undoubtedly will be provided through organized criminal activities. Legally or illegally, their availability in an affluent and increasingly rationalized society is bound to result in their widespread use, both by those who feel deprived of direct experiences that provide sufficient stimulus, novelty, and sensation, and by those exploring the more esoteric fringes of experience. This latter activity is already evident in intellectual circles; it will continue, perhaps under conditions reminiscent of Prohibition.

Avocations and hobbies will abound. Consumption of records, paints, construction kits, tennis rackets, flower seeds, mosaic tiles, classes in Spanish, algebra, and Great Books, hunting and fishing, and whatever else technology brings, will be huge, compared to the past. The more creative pastimes, other than participation in those sports which require imagination and technique, have far to go to become the norm. (8) But even small percents in our large population will mean there will be very many profitable special interest markets. However, in the absence of motives or training for craftsmanship and excellence—ways of life that are not very successfully inculcated in our society as a whole— buying the accouterments of these avocations will be for many the purchase of novelty rather than the beginning of an enlargement and refinement of self. Most who buy these things will actually try them out, and some who bought "something new" will find they have found something more satisfying than mere possession or participation in the latest status fad. Some, of course —and more over time—will, as craftsmen, diligently pursue their avocations. (Very likely these developments will show themselves especially in a growing interest in playing musical instruments, continuing a present trend.) But over the next decade or so, we are not likely to produce a citizenry lavishing craftsmanship and devotion on avocations in proportion to their consumption of the things used in them.

In the second decade there will be more devotion to craftsmanship and excellence as the proportion of younger retired skilled technicians and professionals increases, and as the need for self-enlargement becomes clear enough and time on hand unsatisfying enough to increase the numbers of those who would teach and those who would learn to master some avocation. The change will be for the most part gradual. Nevertheless, the increasing absolute numbers involved will often overload available facilities, as is the case now in national parks and as probably will be the case with adult, college-based, cultural education.

An increasingly critical problem will be how satisfactorily to fill the free time of those who are poor or out of jobs or underemployed. Many of the socially approved forms of recreation and leisure will be little used by them or unavailable to them. In the absence of large-scale ameliorative programs, delinquency, violence, and alienation will be the response of those left out of the affluent life of the next twenty years—a life made all the more attractive and distant for them by its emphasis on leisure and the prerequisite of a job based on skill. It may well be that the government and private organizations will subsidize for these people a kind of adult primary-school system which will mix recreation and the learning of basic thinking tools, knowledge, and social habits. The poverty program's Job Corps presages far larger and more sophisticated programs.

Preoccupation with love and pain in their diverse familiar and deviant forms will continue. The market for both sanctioned and unsanctioned description will be large, and books, illustrations, films, and theatre will become more explicit. There will, of course, be frequent and occasionally effective local attempts to prohibit their distribution, but emphasis on hedonistic consumption, a more casual acceptance of sexual experimenting, exposure to examples in legitimate classical and contemporary literature and art of other nations, the inability of conventional value systems to cope unanimously and consistently with major contemporary issues, the decisions of the courts and the voracious appetites of advertising and entertainment indicate that sex and sadism will be explored more broadly than they are today. Anxieties about sexual adequacy will increase as the insecure and inexperienced of all ages compare their personal behavior with that openly and frequently ascribed to fictional characters. Coping meaningfully and gracefully with this and related issues will be a special challenge for mentors of those who will learn to read well and with comprehension at earlier ages—those who will also be most likely to want to expand their exposure to the adult world.

References

1. Mead, Margaret, "Outdoor Recreation in the Context of Emerging American Cultural Values: Background Considerations," *Trends in American Living and Outdoor Recreation,* Outdoor Recreation Resources Review Commission Report No. 22. Washington, D.C.: U. S. Government Printing Office, 1962, pp. 2–25.

2. Weiss, Robert S., and David Riesman, "Some Issues in the Future of Leisure," *Social Problems,* Vol. IX, No. 1, Society for the Study of Social Problems, Adelphi College, Garden City, New York, Summer 1961, pp. 78–86.

3. American Recreation Foundation, *Work and Free Time in the New Age of Automatic Machines and Computers,* Exploratory Paper No. 1, American Recreation Foundation, Philadelphia, November 1, 1962.

4. "Tourist Project Started in West," New York *Times,* June 25, 1963.

5. Gould, Jack, "Not So Funny—Quality of New TV Season Gives Cause for Considerable Concern," New York Sunday *Times,* October 14, 1962.

6. Wagner, Philip M., "What Makes a Really Good News-

paper and Why They Are So Rare," *Harper's,* Vol. 222, No. 1345, June 1962, p. 12ff.

7. Watts, Allan. *The Joyous Cosmology,* New York: Pantheon, 1962.

8. "Is There a Cultural Explosion?" Washington *Post,* based on recent surveys of the American Institute of Public Opinion, March 3, 1963, p. G–1.

Supplementary References

De Grazia, Sebastian, *Of Time, Work and Leisure.* New York: The Twentieth Century Fund, 1962.

Frank, Lawrence K., Herbert J. Gans, William J. Goode, *et al., Trends in American Living and Outdoor Recreation,* Reports to the Outdoor Recreation Resources Review Commission, No. 22. Washington, D.C.: U. S. Government Printing Office, 1962.

Larrabee, Eric, *The Self-Conscious Society.* New York: Doubleday & Company, Inc., 1960.

—— and Rolf Meyersohn, eds., *Mass Leisure.* New York: The Free Press of Glencoe, Inc., 1958.

Mueller, Eva, and Gerald Gurin, *Participation in Outdoor Recreation: Factors Affecting Demand Among American Adults,* Outdoor Recreation Resources Review Commission Study Report No. 20. Washington, D.C.: U. S. Government Printing Office, 1962.

CHAPTER

12

VALUES AND VIEWPOINTS

THIS CHAPTER is at once a partial review and synthesis of what has gone before and an exploration of factors not conveniently falling into previous chapters. It is concerned with states of mind growing out of and influencing factors discussed earlier. As such, it is concerned with the values and viewpoints surrounding youth in various parts of the adult population. This adult population, which has been alive for at least twenty years, will continue to exert a profound influence over most if not all of the factors affecting youth over the next twenty years. This chapter is concerned, too, with the values of today's youth as they grow from the present into the future, and with the values of the generation of youth which will succeed them, who will not be as much products of the road already traveled as are today's youth. It is also concerned, if only inferentially, with the attitudes, hopes, pettinesses, and greatnesses of those who now have the tasks of planning formal youth development programs. For after all, these people are partially of the past too, though some of those who are youth today should in the near future begin making contributions to such programs: indeed, a few in their teens already are.

Thus, this chapter is a look at the values and viewpoints that grow out of and will influence the factors we have looked at earlier. Values and viewpoints are certainly as important for youth's world as are work and leisure—indeed, more so, since they underlie the choices made in both.

The next twenty years will hold many challenges for prevailing American values and viewpoints. Many of the coming situations are not new ones but the degree and type of reaction to them may be significantly different. More people will be sensitive to issues and circumstances as a result of better education and because, even with no changes in percentages, their absolute numbers will be larger. More people will be personally involved in the outcomes because more issues and circumstances will involve social welfare. Equally important, there will probably be more people for whom these issues and circumstances will have little significance, being removed from personal preoccupations or too complex. The contrast between those who respond to society's challenges and those who do not will have greater political and social consequences for the conduct of democracy and national policy.

The growth in social complexity, which will require increasing rationalization of society, will result in more intense and widespread priority conflicts between traditional community interests. Indeed, part of the issue will be: whose traditional institutional positions are to be preserved and whose changed? Dilemmas will deepen between individual responsibility to conscience and social responsibility to national purpose and to organizational affiliations. International issues involving consequences for the maintenance of peace or the conduct of war will become more amorphous, and the chances will diminish for discovering firm moral positions regarding a given military or political event—especially if, as is likely, brushfire wars, guerrilla actions, and subversion are deliberately encouraged or supported by the United States more frequently. What is morally and ethically right and what is wrong will be perceived differently as the political and social context in which the judgment is made is narrowed or expanded through the information and event-defining sources available to the concerned individual.

The sheer growth in numbers of people—and hence in numbers of events and their consequences—will mean a steadily increasing opportunity to sense the world as full of disaster, crises, violence, danger. For the same reasons there will also be increasing numbers of examples of the safety and support provided in some parts of the world. But these are no more likely to be part of the public image of the world than they now are; the upsetting and disrupting will still provide most of the headlines and spot news interruptions. Putting these events in perspective will mean treating them as percentages. This will bring its own value dilemma (as currently exists in the prototype of future public-issue dilemmas: does one evaluate bomb-testing fallout in terms of the *per-cent* increase in tragedies or in terms of the increased *number* of tragedies?).

These deepening dilemmas of interpretation and action will lead to more polarization of personal solutions. Some will find themselves searching more deeply for a moral basis for action: some will find a moral basis for dogmatism, some for relativism. Some will opt out, turning to private preoccupations. Others, especially among those who rise to power, will obsessively pursue the same techniques which we like to think have produced our successes: the calculated manipulation of environment and man by the exploitation of technology and organization.

DISPOSSESSION, POTENCY, AND PARTICIPATION AMONG ADULTS

As the next two decades proceed, a larger proportion of adults, especially older ones, will find themselves dispossessed in one way or another of lifelong jobs, of favored views or ideas, of a sense of being in close touch with what is happening to man and his world. Whereas more of the younger generation than in the past will, to a somewhat greater extent, be brought up to expect dispossession in one form or another, older adults will not as a group adjust easily to this. For them, anxiety, depression, annoyance, and hostility arising from felt incompetence and in reaction to being pulled out of deep ruts, will accompany forced changes in jobs and viewpoints. By and large, people in middle life and older don't like to change the way they have been doing and seeing things—especially if the change is required in the midst of economic and social insecurity.

This sense of dispossession will be especially frustrating because its sources will be exceedingly difficult to "get at" by conventional political methods. The scientists, technicians, and rationalizers will be deep in the interstices of the bureaucracies of government and industry, their products and programs based on esoteric equations and computer programs and on the subtle jargons of the natural and social sciences.

Unless these changes are made in ways that take into account the emotional needs of those being dispossessed, there will be resistance to them. Indeed, we can expect the older groups to exert political pressures intended to protect themselves from either the experience or the consequences of material, ideological, or emotional dispossession. The growing size and political potency of this older group will confront the nation with priority conflicts over how to meet the economic, social, and physical needs of both youth and older generations.

At the same time, much of the well-educated younger generation and the older, versatile, and well-trained professional group will be happy with or, at least, indifferent to the high rate of change. For many, the world will be as inspiring and as full of opportunity, by virtue of the rate of change, as it will for others be a source of despair.

For most of that population which concerns itself with attention to public issues, the trend will be toward feeling less and less competent to understand or influence larger national and international problems. In part, this will be due to a heightened realization of the overwhelming range of events as conveyed by expanded mass media. In part, it will be due to the inability of those who try to remain alert and involved in the issues to keep up with the rapid and interacting social and technological changes that will define these issues. In part, it will be caused by a growing sense of being locked into a system so complex and so large that the individual (including many so-called leaders) cannot understand it, much less affect its operation. Many will recognize that the intellectual prerequisites will be great indeed for effective participation in the idea-producing, decision-making, policy-planning activities at top levels of big institutions. Not very many who have more leisure

time, then, are likely to spend it wrestling with these relatively abstract issues when so many opportunities for
direct experience will be readily available.

Probably one victim of the period ahead will be a
"sense of history." As Kenneth Keniston puts it, describing the plight of some of today's youth: ". . . the past
grows more remote and irrelevant psychologically . . .
the future grows more remote and unpredictable . . .
the present assumes a new significance as the one time
in which the environment is relevant, immediate and
knowable." (1) The same will hold for many of tomorrow's adults, especially the better educated who, in
earlier days, would have looked to history for insight.
For many, even the present will seem so subject to alternative interpretations that it will tend to lack the
definitiveness expected of events that "go down in history." Among the most sophisticated it will be understood that events often will lack definitiveness even for
those making history: such will be the complexity and
pace of events that whatever records there are will, in
important ways, often be inadequate for future histori-
cal interpretation. How the teaching of history will be
tied to this kind of present remains to be worked out.

For those not particularly aware of issues except when
they become crises (of which there will be a continuing
supply, some real and some locally contrived to meet
the demand for novelty and sensation), the continuing
international and national dangers, frustrations, and difficulties will probably heighten feelings of generalized,
unfocused uneasiness, shorten time perspectives, and
amplify needs for evidences of personal sure-footedness.
The latter will be sought chiefly through the consumption
of things and symbols, especially in connection with increasing opportunities for leisure-time activities.

Nevertheless, given the strong tendencies of most people to make sense of the world in ways compatible with what they already believe, the views and values of much of the adult population are unlikely to be subject to far-reaching changes, except possibly in emphasis, over the next several years. Most of their time, the majority of adults will, as now, be almost unaware of the complexities of this world. When events coalesce into headlines, they will interpret and evaluate the issues in terms of their conventional values and beliefs about self, nation, right and wrong, and "the other guy," transforming the complexities of policy and events into the equivalent of everyday household, interpersonal experiences.

Some of those who can cope with the complexity of values and events will continue to try to make sense out of and take action on national and international issues. They will also find themselves increasingly incapable of discovering adequate syntheses for what is happening, or values sufficient to meet the ambiguity and amorphousness that will characterize this world. Those who need to pursue their values or relieve their frustrations and sense of disconnectedness through action will increasingly do so through involvement in very local civic and political issues and through participation in voluntary service organizations where the values involved will be familiar and malleable.

Others in this group will seek a sense of solidity and adequacy of viewpoint by avoiding involvement in the big issues, or crises, turning instead to intense interpersonal and private experiences such as love, sex, religion, hallucinatory drugs, art, teaching, and other individual and small-group activities that stress the immediate, personal experience of self.

Others, aware of changing circumstances, needing a rigid framework of values for coping with them, will commit themselves to extremist groups. In particular, many people, particularly older adults, will seek evidences of sure-footedness by supporting conservative and reactionary causes and philosophies. They will espouse traditional and pseudo-traditional viewpoints emphasizing ideas and actions, which they will see as means for producing a world in which they can again be potent. During this period some late adolescents and young adults who feel dispossessed will make common cause with the older disaffected.

VIEWPOINTS OF YOUTH

A growing group (at least, insofar as the numbers in this age group will be growing) of the most talented, sensitive, and searching of young adults and adolescents will be repelled by what they interpret as politicking, commercialism, high-pressure bureaucracy, and the "big" society, and by logic and the esoteric, "dehumanized" and "hemmed-in" experience of the devoted scientist. (2) They will seek expression and careers in the arts, the humanities; in teaching in primary and secondary schools; in social service in the emerging nations and at home; in organized and unorganized political action social protest, and so on. Uncynical commitment to an uncorrupted task will be their goal. They will also turn intensively to self-emphasizing experiences with love, family, sex, religion, hallucinatory drugs, and so on. These youth will often make very necessary and very important social contributions, but thereby some of our best talent will be exported or otherwise unavailable for other social tasks where precisely this sensitivity will be much needed. This "skill" shortage will become more serious, too, over the next twenty years.

Another group of the well educated will, as they al-

ways have, be undaunted by the ambiguities and con-
tradictions of the times will be aiming for and beginning
to move into management and politics, manipulating
men and events to serve pragmatic goals.

A third group will move into the professions, and
more or less submerge their value conflicts and the
events engendering them under the pressures, constraints, and attractions of professional competition and
accomplishment.

The rest—that is, most adolescents becoming adults
during the next ten years—will not be much better or
worse as citizens than their recent predecessors; their
cultural pedigrees will not be essentially different from
those of today. The trends surveyed suggest that during
the second decade a substantially larger proportion of
young people will fall into the above three categories,
but how the proportions will be allocated depends on
the actual rate and distribution of other changes discussed—to say nothing of those overlooked.

Those adolescents and young adults exposed to conventional levels of education and occupations in the
next decade, including those who develop as a new
class of skilled technicians, will have less interest than
the highly educated in the problems of the times and
less ability to confront them at a significant level of understanding of self and society. They will not be devoid
of values and beliefs any more than their equivalents
are today, but their viewpoints will not be much more
adequate than they are today for deeply understanding
the world and their place in it.

The adolescents and young adults who are relatively
poorly educated or who receive almost no education
will increasingly develop their own values and beliefs,
justifying withdrawal from or violence toward the rest of

society. Here, unorganized crime will continue to flourish and, probably, will increase. Without enormous and carefully planned and programed efforts, it will become steadily more difficult to convince these people it is in their interest and within their ability to share the values and viewpoints of the society which has so grievously deprived them. (3)

ETHNIC VIEWPOINTS

Ethnic identity, an important factor in American politics, will gradually lose its potency over the next two decades. Among the older workers now living in ethnic communities some dispersal will occur when, retrained, they move to other areas where jobs, but not necessarily ethnic-based neighborhoods, will be found. Pressures for joint urban attacks on regional problems will provide political excuses to set aside first consideration to ethnic interests and attitudes. The first generation of college students from ethnic communities will find these ties weakened as they take on occupational and social identities with less parochial perspectives. Implicit in this development will be the further attenuation of attachment to the past, to history—even ethnically oriented history. Also implicit probably will be greater freedom of choice for Federal foreign policy, unfettered by concern for ethnic bloc votes.

IMAGE OF MAN

During the next two decades, belief in man as unique in himself and in his relation to the rest of the universe will, in many of the influential decision-making and policy-planning levels of society, become substantially secondary to viewing him as subject to the same manipulation and attention as other dynamic parts of social and physical systems. Certain developments in science and technology will contribute to this state of mind, as will other social factors discussed in this report.

Medical technology intimately linking man with machinery, some ability to replace organs with machinery or with those of another person, and specific and general-purpose drugs for maintaining health and curing sickness will continue to remove the mystery from at least the more prevalent maladies. The body will increasingly be accepted as maintainable and repairable, much as any fine piece of equipment which is cared for by "preventive maintenance" and through specific repair.

Emphasis on human engineering and on precise training so man and machine can work well and comfortably together will emphasize man as a biomechanical link. The growing use of chemicals in special situations to control moods and mental efficiency will add to this image. Finally, the synthesis of life in primitive forms and possibly the discovery of life forms on Mars will, for some, subtract from the mystery of life by making it less unique.

There will also be an increasingly vocal body of informed opinion asserting that man is infinitely more than a manipulable thing and that, indeed, our troubles stem from treating him as if that were all he is. But lip service to man's uniqueness may well ease reluctance to treat him otherwise. (This ritual acknowledgment is already part of many government and business policy-planning papers and program reports.) It is hard to see, however, how this "antimanipulation" viewpoint could be incorporated into the growingly popular

statistical approach based on computer-oriented rationalization, or how it could significantly change the viewpoints of those exhilarated by the opportunity to apply
economics, behavioral science, systems analysis, and
computer methods to the social processes. Over the long
run, as unhappy experience leads to understanding that
rationalization involves more than logic and computer-
encompassable efficiency, this humanistic viewpoint may
begin to carry real weight. The long run may come
about late in the period we are talking about. (We will
return to the possibility that those who argue for the
broader view of man will find a larger audience among
the dispossessed, disaffected, and disemployed.)

MANIPULATION OF THE SOCIAL
ENVIRONMENT

The emphasis on manipulation of the environment, the
growing treatment of man as a thing within the environment, and the quantification (both pseudo and real) of
the behavioral sciences will encourage the application
of social engineering wherever fad and practicability
make it useful to do so. It will be practiced—and sometimes corrupted—by behavioral engineers, as well as
by others who seek to influence various publics for various purposes, although not all the purposes will be evil
by any means. After all, the needed programs we have
spoken of will require the cultivation of public support. The behavioral sciences will also be oversold, not
so much by the scientists as by those who want them to
do the job. In most cases, during the next decade at
least, the results will not be as conclusive as those who
use them would hope. But this will not stop most people
from believing they have been manipulated—or stop

many from believing that such manipulation is desirable and socially necessary in many circumstances.

Nevertheless, growing acceptance of the manipulation of man will encourage the careful application of valid behavioral science methods and facts to social problems. As has been the case with the application of other expertise, interpretations from the behavioral sciences will often be employed to emphasize or to obscure issues so that, while used more, the behavioral sciences will only occasionally be the final arbiter of policy in the next decade.

During the 1970's, the behavioral sciences will probably be applied and effective to about the extent that economics is today (and will probably be no more internally schismatic than today's economic theory and practice). Their accumulating record of success in business and in the military will legitimize their application to many national problems. For by 1970 we will have to face truly critical problems in education, urban development, public-opinion manipulation and political-economic warfare, and only the behavioral sciences (often combined with economics) will have the expertise to deal with them.

It is not unlikely that the philosophy of law will be influenced by the factors we have discussed. In particular, the growth of knowledge about the wellsprings of behavior and the general trend toward rationalization will encourage, in the appropriate areas, the increasing application of law as a means to individual therapy in and to potency for deprived groups. Emphasis on abundance rather than scarcity, on consumption rather than possession, may be reflected in some changing views about the meaning of property. (4)

ATTITUDES TOWARD EXPERTS
AND ISSUES

Natural science and technology will grow as a perva-
sive and powerful lobby for their own interests, emphasizing a manipulative and rational approach to society and its problems. Inevitably, this lobby and its
supporters will make intensive use of public relations to
sell itself to those publics, decision-makers, and opinion-makers who will listen. The already evident dis-
quiet among some scientists and laymen will deepen as
the struggle between disinterested and "political" science and technology factions becomes more intense.
(5) Respect for facts and for the means for discovering
them will remain high, though corruptible; indeed, the
consumers of science and technology will themselves
gradually become more respectful of the integrity of
facts. But although the growing influence of scientists
and engineers is a precursor of the mind-oriented world
of work, some of these professionals have shared and
more frequently will come to share some of the operating
values and goals of their beneficiaries and sources of support—government, industry, and the military. As the
tasks of scientists and engineers become more closely
tied to the goals of their clients, interpretation of the
facts and defense of the interpretation will become more
subject to the values of their nonscientist clients. (6)
Then, too, competing interpretations of the facts and
"competing" facts (because their relationship to each
other is not understood) and facts about the limits
or meaning of other facts will frequently produce exceedingly complex communications problems and encourage oversimplification and self-justifying selection

and emphasis. Scientists have never been unemotional, unbiased, and unfailingly ethical in defending their interpretations of facts. In the future, these human weaknesses will be more evident outside the science community, in part because the behavior will be more prevalent within it, and in part because other segments of the science community will be deeply and vocally concerned with the ethical problems engendered.

On major issues, the conflicting positions of experts and the arguments they use to defend themselves will be more exposed as an increasingly large educated audience makes it economically sensible for some of the media to air them. But it is very likely that the arguments, except in one's own specialty, will demonstrate the inability of the nonexpert to contribute to the resolution of the issues or to convince himself that he knows what the answers (or, often, the questions) really are. Today's debates about fallout, defense policy, insecticides, and manned-space efforts typify what is to come. When the questions involve national policy, the conscientious voter who knows he doesn't know for sure will find his democratic obligation a particularly frustrating one.

That issues will be subtle, complex, and interrelated will not discourage some from making them "causes." One way of dealing with a sense of being overwhelmed and dispossessed will undoubtedly be to join causes. From time to time a popular cause will force or channel government action, especially if the cause derives from economic deprivation. But, although the increased media outlets will make it easier for groups to get their message "out," it is not at all clear that such messages will be very influential. (It is not at all clear that such messages are often very influential now!) Most causes will probably tend to become chiefly a means for preserving the *forms* of popular democracy at the citizen level.

Those insufficiently educated to appreciate the nature of the controversies are no more likely to be aroused by them than they are now. But as the media report on an increasing number of important topics, many of which are subjects of controversy by experts, those with mediocre education will feel even more a sense of being left out and incompetent to deal with the issues which they recognize as somehow defining their lives and futures. A means for coping with these feelings will be cynicism about the utility of experts in general, and belief, often well founded, that "experts have their rackets just like everybody else." It may also be that if these people feel sufficiently left out and frustrated about the issues they feel they have a stake in, they will find their own spokesmen, who will speak in simpler terms uncomplicated by conflicting facts or the vested interests of the parties arguing at higher levels.

Among those already adult today there will be, of course, large numbers who will remain or grow indifferent to these controversies. Active cynicism or resentment or indifference toward the technical issues on the part of some people and real, if frustrated, concern with the issues in others will deepen the difficulties for policy-makers of contriving meaningful and useful decisions calculated to strengthen and preserve democratic processes.

THE PLACE OF WOMEN

Concern and dissatisfaction with the functional and emotional place of women in this society will increase, because larger numbers of women and men will have the backgrounds that foster such concern. This concern will be more focused, because more educated women will have time for careers and skilled service as their families grow up, and there will be greater competition with men for unskilled jobs. Moreover, there will be more conflict between the emphasis on rationalization and on the "intuitive," "human" approach to life which will continue to be the chief avenue for creative participation open to many women. Many more experiments will be aimed at getting women out of the home or at keeping them happy in it. Some of these will be successful, but it is most unlikely that the actions undertaken will be sufficient to solve over-all the problem of meaningful life for women in the next two decades. (7) Major changes in popularly accepted roles for women, which will be emotionally rewarding and socially beneficial, will wait for changes in the definition of male roles and in the ways society allocates its affluence. The changes will have to be incorporated into female education and into occupational and child-raising institutions. The consequences of such redefinitions will be realized even later.

THE UNDERPRIVILEGED

In the next few years, the contrast between the deprived and poverty-stricken portion of our population and that enjoying a high standard of living will present a blatant challenge to our egalitarian ethos. The distinctions made between those who cannot or will not and those who can and do, based ever more on the ability to bring good and trained minds and hands to bear on progressively more complex problems, will gradually emphasize that this is becoming an elite society with the prizes going to those best endowed and best trained.

The rapidly increasing burden of humanely coping with the economically unproductive and the mentally underendowed (not to mention the many other problems that sheer human numbers will generate at home and abroad), will subtly begin to affect attitudes about the value and purpose of the individual life. Some will find in these serious situations deeper commitment to belief in the integrity and value of the individual. Others will more and more base their interpretations of the value of human beings on statistical measures, on their utility for alternative social "pay-offs." (This kind of thinking is applied by some today to national defense considerations and to deriving "acceptable" levels of human loss of life in nuclear war.) The dilemmas inherent in either standard of evaluation are likely to deepen as the era moves on.

It is plausible that over this time period the occupationally, socially, and emotionally dispossessed will produce their own intense reaction. Whether this group can or will be organized into a potent pressure group remains to be seen. The effectiveness of the Negro boycotts and other nonviolent actions in the South indicates one trend. That the antiwhite, separationist, armageddonist Black Muslims are a fast-growing religious group in the United States is indicative of another trend. Others of these dispossessed could add support to the various rigid, extremist action groups already seeking a simpler world.

RELIGION

The number of churchgoers probably will increase more or less as the population does, but probably not at the astonishing rates, which from World War II until 1962 exceeded the rate of population increase. (8) Church membership will continue to offer periodically needed feelings of spiritual unity, "in-groupness," shared values, sociability, and identity with national aspirations—at least to the extent these are perceived as preserving the same things that the religions stand for. (9) Churchgoing is most unlikely to produce a country more morally or ethically united on a system of values applicable to the domestic and international problems which confront our citizens, laymen, and church leaders alike. It will provide a sense of support, a deity to depend upon, but it is not likely to inspire in most a dedication to seeking and expressing God with truly felt religious spirit. Richard Carter summarizes a *Good Housekeeping* magazine Consumer Panel Survey on religion this way:

The survey reveals a majority outlook full of extraordinary contrasts: almost everyone practices a formal religion, but the individual, whatever his affiliation may be, is likely to be less attuned to and less concerned about the hereafter than might be expected; church attendance is at an all-time high, but an amazing number of those who go to church do not believe that attendance is essential to upright living; most people pray, but the prayers are more likely to express self-concern than self-sacrifice. (10)

The philosophical, moral, and human problems explored at high levels of sophisticated theological discourse will be too esoteric to have meaning for the average churchgoer. (11) The conventional forms of religious, moral, and ethical dogma, as well as their looser interpretations, will continue to compete with the countervailing values and accepted behavior of daily life, or they will be warped or used expeditiously in the pursuit of secular aims. Ministers, priests, and rabbis will continue to make pronouncements about the right and wrong of public and private conduct. But their own understanding of national and international issues will, in many cases, be no more sophisticated than that of their flocks. Even when their understanding of both the secular and theological issues is deep, secular considerations often will discourage outspokenness.

This is not to say that major religions will be powerless either to affect the individual or to influence local and national policy. Probably there will be numerically more groups of deeply religious people trying through religion to give direction to secular life or to avoid its confrontations. Probably there will be numerically more outspoken religious leaders willing to risk for their consciences the disapproval of their congregations and religious bureaucracies. Such actions will sometimes alter the course of local events. Doubtless, religious groups will continue to make important contributions to social welfare. And evangelical movements and "store front" churches will not lose their appeal, especially if the numbers of economically and socially dispossessed increase. But the power and influence of the major religious denominations in the next two decades will not be substantially greater or less than today. Local religious leaders will seldom be able to bring the issues of the spirit to bear on the daily actions of private citizens and public figures. For just as today, it will be too distracting in the marketplace to reconcile God with a rationalizing society.

If the social and economic problems we have pointed out grow to crisis proportions and are not adequately dealt with, a leader might well arise who will draw together those intellectually dissatisfied and economically dispossessed, looking for an ideology, a religion, which will give the sense of commitment and belonging. What the nature of the doctrine might be is moot.

In keeping with the general industrialized world view, which sees merit in cooperative action and its facilitation through large institutional aggregations, the drawing together of the major Christian churches will probably slowly continue. The chances are good that for many years to come any impact of ecumenicism on political action or religious commitment will be small. The ultimate effect on American religious practice and social action cannot profitably be conjectured, since there are no indications of what dogma or organization will evolve. If the efforts of the Vatican and a mellowing of the USSR bring about some sort of rapprochement, a less intransigent attitude in the Catholic bloc is likely to result. This, in turn, would increase the negotiating flexibility of various governments.

SCIENTIFIC THEORIES

Given the inherent radicalness of major new theoretical formulations in science, one cannot speculate on their specific impact on values and viewpoints. One cannot even hazard a forecast about whether they will occur during the time period here considered or, if they do, what fields of knowledge they will encompass. Perhaps the present impasse in understanding the nature of matter will be overcome. Perhaps biological processes will be reformulated in a more unified manner. Possibly, a powerful overarching theory of social behavior will be invented. What *can* be suggested, however, is that the theories will be—as powerful new theories always are—so alien to conventional levels of perception and understanding that their influence on world views will be relatively limited for a number of years. Undoubtedly, they will be vulgarized as were those of Freud and Einstein, and in the very popularizing the newness will be corrupted, perhaps dangerously, into conventionality plus novelty.

For most people tomorrow, even as today: As far as their own lives are concerned or the deep issues of their relations to nature or an ultimate power, they are able to see nothing that is shocking and little that is illuminating or helpful. The really big news comes to them faintly, more and more faintly "like the dwindling shouts of a search party that has disappeared into an enormous maze." (12)

Some new concepts may spread faster than in the past among intellectuals and, since this group will be growing larger, the ideas will be more widely dispersed. But the practical products of the theories will have more impact for some years than will the radical shift in world view implicit in them.

INTERNATIONAL VIEWPOINTS

Living outside the United States for a few months, or even for many years, will become far more common in the next twenty years. More money, cheaper and more convenient travel arrangements, and many more opportunities to live, learn, and give service will be available through foreign aid programs, activities like the Peace Corps, and university exchange programs, as well as through business and industrial expansion into other nations. The simple quest for novelty and new experience will attract even more people.

For those with the education and the sensitivity to respond to their experience, world travel will emphasize the relativity of values and standards of social behavior and the profound differences in living standards between the United States and the underdeveloped areas. For some, their experiences will further weaken conventional values and viewpoints. For others, the diversity and complexity experienced will entrench attachments to what they believe to be traditional American values and to nationalistic orientations. Many, of course, will simply find the foreign country a diversion, and they will so little sense the differences that they will return to the United States with their values or views unaltered. Many will, through these experiences, develop a broader and deeper sense of the strengths and weaknesses of humanity.

The point here is that the number of those so influenced will grow, rather than that the influences will be different from those produced today. More students, intellectuals, and professionals will travel to other countries, as will more people who have no special credentials other than money. Aware of the differences between cultures, more relatively important people will come to greater acceptance of the existence and legitimacy of differences in goals and life styles. This acceptance should reduce support for extremist and chauvinistic perspectives at home. For at least the next decade, however, this group will not reflect the views of the majority of the population, who will not have had the broadening experience of world travel except vicariously (and highly selectively) via TV and the movies. Nevertheless, these people will build a basis for influencing leadership and youth toward a more meaningful internationalism. During the 1970's and 1980's, such perspectives may be overridden by domestic and international frustration.

Other direct and indirect consequences of exposure

to peoples and products of other nations will also challenge conventional viewpoints. In the first place, it will gradually be borne in on people preoccupied with the problems of youth that some of the most dramatic and successful experiments in youth development are under way in the emerging nations. Most important, youth themselves play a major and often decisive role in planning and implementing the programs. (13) Moreover, very young leaders will be far more prevalent in these countries than in ours. The great usefulness and high status of youth in these countries, in contrast to our inability to decide what we want from our young people, may encourage more imaginative experiments here in youth development.

In the second place, the expansion of international trade and the growing ability of the highly developed nations to produce a large variety and great quantity of consumer items will gradually enlarge some consumers' sense of the world they can draw on. The economic challenge represented by these products will produce in some a growing sense of dependency on and involvement with other nations.

In the third place, growing cultural exchange will engender a greater sense of world community, even in those who are more interested in being entertained than in being international.

In the fourth place, as the African and Asian nations come more to express national intentions in terms of their native secular and religious values, there will be a gradual impingement on American minds of standards of conduct, belief, and values other than those of the Judeo-Christian tradition. In a few generations, technicians and managers from all societies will come to hold similar standards because they will have similar operating problems, means, and goals. But in the next two decades the transition will be full of shocks and frictions for many, and exciting enlargements in perspective for others.

References

1. Keniston, Kenneth, "Social Change and Youth in America," in Stephen R. Graubard, ed., *Daedalus, Youth: Change and Challenge.* Vol. 91, No. 1, American Academy of Arts and Sciences, Winter 1962, pp. 152–153.

2. Goodman, Paul, *Growing Up Absurd.* New York: Random House, Inc., 1956.

3. Moles, Oliver, Ronald Lippitt, and Stephen Withey, *A Selective Review of Research and Theory on Delinquency.* Survey Research Center, Institute for Social Research, University of Michigan, Ann Arbor, Mich., 1959.

4. McDonald, Donald, Edward Bennett Williams, and Bethuel M. Webster, *The Law.* Santa Barbara, Calif.: Center for the Study of Democratic Institutions, 1962.

5. Stover, Carl F., *The Government of Science.* Santa Barbara, Calif.: Center for the Study of Democratic Institutions, 1962.

6. Wohlstetter, Albert, "Scientists, Seers and Strategy," *Foreign Affairs,* Vol. 41, No. 3, Council on Foreign Relations, Inc., April 1963, pp. 466–478.

7. "The American Female," *Harper's,* A Special Supplement, John Fischer, ed., Vol. CCXXV, No. 1349, October 1962.

8. Landis, Benson Y., ed., *The Yearbook of American Churches, 1963,* Vol. 31, Published by the National Council of the Churches of Christ.

9. Kluckhohn, Clyde, "Have There Been Discernible Shifts in American Values During the Past Generation?" in Elting E. Morison, ed., *The American Style.* New York: Harper & Row, 1958, p. 145.

10. Carter, Richard, "What Women *Really* Think About Religion . . . ," *Good Housekeeping* Special Report, January 1963, pp. 58–59, 149–152.

11. Robinson, John A. T., *Honest to God.* Philadelphia: Westminster Press, 1963; and Edwards, David L., ed., *The Honest to God Debate.* Philadelphia: Westminster Press, 1963.

12. Heckscher, August, *The Public Happiness*. New York: Atheneum, 1962, p. 14.

13. *Way Forum and Way Review*. World Assembly of Youth, 66 Rue Saint Bernard, Brussels, Belgium.

Supplementary References

Bell, Daniel, *The End of Ideology: On the Exhaustion of Political Ideas in the Fifties*. New York: Collier Books, new, rev. ed., 1962.

"America, Mass Society, and Mass Media," *The Journal of Social Issues*, Bennis, Warren G., Issue Editor, Vol. 16, No. 3, Society for the Psychological Study of Social Issues, Ann Arbor, 1960.

Cloward, Richard A., and Lloyd E. Ohlin, *Delinquency and Opportunity*. New York: The Free Press of Glencoe, Inc., 1960.

Coleman, James S., *The Adolescent Society*. New York: The Free Press of Glencoe, Inc., 1961.

De Jouvenel, Bertrand, "The Political Consequences of the Rise of Science," *Bulletin of the Atomic Scientists*, December 1963, pp. 2–8.

The Elite and the Electorate: Is Government by the People Possible? Santa Barbara, Calif.: Center for the Study of Democratic Institutions, 1963.

Gallup, George, and Evan Hill, "Youth, the Cool Generation," *The Saturday Evening Post*, Combined issues December 23 and 30, 1961, pp. 63–80.

Keniston, Kenneth, "American Students and the 'Political Revival'," *The American Scholar*, Vol. 32, No. 1, 1962, pp. 40–64.

Lane, Robert E., *Political Ideology*. New York: The Free Press of Glencoe, Inc., 1962.

Lyford, Joseph P., *The Talk in Vandalia*. New York: Fund for the Republic, 1962.

"Mass Culture and Mass Media," *Daedalus*, Gerald Holton, ed., American Academy of Arts and Sciences, Spring 1960.

Mazoo, Earl, Malcolm Moos, Hallock Hoffman, and Harvey Wheeler, *The Great Debates*. Santa Barbara, Calif.: Center for the Study of Democratic Institutions, 1962, pp. 8, 14, 16.

Riesman, David, *Individualism Reconsidered*. New York: The Free Press of Glencoe, Inc., 1954.

———, Nathan Glazer, and Denney Reuel, *The Lonely Crowd, A Study of the Changing American Character*. New Haven: Yale University Press, 1961, rev. ed.

"Science and Technology in Contemporary Society," *Daedalus*, Gerald Holton, ed., American Academy of Arts and Sciences, Spring 1962.

SECTION

IV

In Summary

WE CAN EXPECT technology to provide a growing capability for manipulating both the material environment and human behavior. Technology should provide a further capacity to preserve and extend life and a growing variety of objects with which to enjoy it, or at least to preoccupy ourselves during it. In particular, we can expect cybernation to increase enormously our material goods and our ability to collect, process, and use information. This ability will encourage greater control over the management, planning, and implementation of social processes. The potential for major developments in housing and recreation is implicit in certain technological advances. Our local and domestic communications capacity will increase hugely. Large engineering research and development programs may well require international cooperation.

Crises likely will arise in education, unemployment, retraining, urban development, recreation facilities, and support for the aged and underendowed. Greater efforts will be required to deal with these increasingly complex issues. Population growth will itself generate welfare problems, for even small percentages of deprivation or dispossession will represent large numbers of people.

This increasingly technological, complex, and large society will raise the premium on skilled minds. The need will also increase for skilled craftsmen to develop and maintain everything from computers to garbage disposals. Neither skilled hands nor well-trained minds are likely to be available in the quality and quantity needed to meet the multiple critical national needs—or to fully develop national luxuries. Middle-level professional and managerial personnel and skilled blue-collar workers, who will be displaced by cybernation, will add to the potential pool of needed skilled, but retraining them will by no means be simple. Emotional insecurity and trained incapacity are not easy to overcome.

Urban problems will become steadily more complicated as communities expand into megalopoli. Although conventional political structures will prove inadequate for meeting them, strong political pressures will inhibit the growth of regional governments. Encouraged by Federal support contingent on the use of problem-oriented approaches, these problems will be attacked (though too often piecemeal) chiefly through such devices as multicity "Authorities." The growth of central-city Negro populations will result in Negro political control in some of them.

The backlog and growing supply of the relatively unskilled and unemployed will present enormous problems for both research and action. Of special importance will be the problem of providing meaningful jobs and social status for the underprivileged from urban and rural slums. Persistence of a population of deprived and unemployed Negroes, exacerbated by their increased numbers, will present a tremendous challenge to national morality and social well-being.

Providing means for training the unskilled female work force and for motivating young women to seek high school and college educations which will let them make a much needed contribution to the economic and social development of the nation will also be a formidable problem.

Planning educations for occupations will be more difficult because of lack of sufficient foreknowledge about specific occupational needs as they are altered by rapid technological change. Blue-collar, white-collar, managerial, and professional personnel alike will be affected, though in different ways. At all levels, insufficient numbers of guidance counselors with insufficient understanding of the nature of the new job opportunities will make it additionally difficult for youth to choose well.

Although the general level of factual education will improve, it will improve more for those from the better and wealthier schools. In the kind of world we are moving into, the differences between the "haves" and the "have lesses" and the "have nots" will increase, even though the conditions of the latter two will improve somewhat as compared to present standards. One expression of this difference will be a growing tendency to cultivate an elite of "social servants" who, by virtue of their wits, drive, and aspirations, will be given a deeper and more stringent education at each level of schooling. The pressures to choose careers which exploit talent and aptitudes will increase, and more students will find themselves more anxious, more competitive, more "hemmed-in" earlier in their education. One way or another, more people will continue their education for work and leisure during more of their life than ever before.

For some years at least, most youth will not find at home, in school, or in any other institution that helps to guide them a set of values that will significantly reduce the present confusion and over-all inadequacy of perspectives, standards, aspirations, and goals. Most people will probably not be much better able to participate in the resolution of society's problems than they are now, and the percentage interested in doing so will not be much greater. Indeed, the gap between the concerned and the indifferent is likely to enlarge.

Leisure time for skilled technicians, be they technologists or service personnel, will, on the whole, increase. Gradually, the variety of productive leisure-time activities will increase too. The arts, both professional and amateur, are very likely to have a renaissance. Active recreational participation will continue to grow. So, too, will spectator activities, especially as recreational facilities become more crowded. However, for many, waiting for access to such facilities will itself come to occupy a substantial amount of nonwork time.

In the underdeveloped parts of the world there will be years of turmoil with, generally speaking, little improvement in living standards, with trends toward authoritarian governments, and with rising resentment toward leadership that does not provide quick improvements, and toward the rich, developed nations.

The USSR will probably become a more important economic and political competitor, and there is a fair chance that military power will become less important in our dealings with each other. Relations with China are likely to become more fluid, but not necessarily better.

The threat of mutual annihilation will not quickly disappear and the numbers and varieties of local and clandestine wars may increase.

Our relations with our allies, especially in Europe, will be more or less amicable, if delicate, as Europe becomes more and more independent economically and politically and, thereby, more likely to have goals and programs not necessarily compatible with ours. In the long run we will find ourselves still closely identified with them. The growing strength of the European economic community is likely to require greater economic efficiencies in the United States and, possibly, establishment of trade alliances with non-European nations.

The actions of the UN will become less frequently congruent with our national interests. At the same time the proliferation of international agencies in which we as a nation have a deep involvement will increase, as will the number of international activities involving private enterprises and institutions.

As business and government grow in size and mutual dependence, the distinctions between the two will become more blurred. If, as seems likely, there are large government public-works programs using the unskilled unemployed, this tendency will be accelerated. The transition to an economy less dependent on the arms industry (if likely major steps in arms control and disarmament occur) will also require very close meshing of government and business.

More and more social and economic problems will have to be dealt with as national problems: the pressure will be strong to rationalize many kinds of management and planning operations, especially in government. This trend will be encouraged by a combination of other trends: skill shortages, growingly complex welfare problems, the powers of the computer to simulate events and to provide information based on enormous amounts of data, increasingly sophisticated and valid models of social behavior, and increasing utilization of physical and social scientists and engineers. People will not necessarily be forced into bleak conformity, although in the short run rationalization may well mean more emphasis on doing what the "plan" says, sacrificing second-thought originality to program continuity. The rationalization of activities will be gradual and need not deprive most holdouts for individuality and spontaneous behavior. Outside of the work environment there will be many opportunities for spontaneity and whimsy.

Shortages of skilled personnel, the profoundly critical nature of some of our coming social welfare problems, and improved techniques of rationalization will gradually lead to the establishment of explicit national priorities and, thereby, to the balancing of potential major skill-using projects against the social welfare needs of the nation. At one time or another this is bound to pain various major interests. In the process of working out these priorities, scientists and engineers will become more active and more recognized as advocates with other commitments than the stereotypic disinterested truth-seeking and manipulation of the material environment.

Other trends, having to do with the citizen's continuing loss of value "anchor points" and with his indifference to many domestic and international issues, are likely to encourage public and private procrastinations and partial, often counterproductive, actions. In particular, it will take time to effect major changes in education, the treatment of delinquents, retraining for the unskilled and for women, and so on, on a large scale, since such a scale will be costly and politically controversial. For many new approaches the sort of strong arguments which research and carefully evaluated pilot projects could provide will be necessary. But it will take several years to prepare, undertake, interpret, and apply the findings from these studies, and further years for the results to show.

These speculations may sound as if the socioeconomic characteristics of the population during the next two decades will be very much like those of the present: there will be the well educated, the semieducated, and the uneducated; the wealthy, the well-to-do, the poor, and the poverty-stricken; the elites and the masses. This of course, is so, at least during the next two decades, simply because this society, in the context of world society, is very unlikely to change fundamentally or obliterate these categories (unless there are disastrous or magnificent unforeseen events or personalities—which cannot be planned for anyway). But much more is being said which is worth emphasizing in this summary.

During the next two decades, growing social, technological, and scientific complexity, turmoil in the emerging nations, delicate problems with our allies, and sheer population growth will put an even greater premium on the most highly trained and superior manual and intellectual abilities. The kind of training for meeting these conditions will emphasize the techniques of learning and unlearning, attitudes of craftsmanship and commitment, and technical proficiency. To be fully effective, this training will have to be introduced early and pervasively into the child's experience and practiced throughout life. It is especially important to realize that on the basis of our present understanding of the processes involved in becoming a responsible and responsive social being, it is unlikely that during the next ten to twenty years we will, *on the wholesale and articulated scale required,* reorient the motives, skills, and aspirations of the underprivileged adolescent or adult so he may join as an equal those so trained since childhood. This raises enormous problems in the light of the disproportionately large Negro population likely to be in this category. It also raises enormous problems regarding the social roles of the mentally underendowed.

As now, those already privileged will more easily provide the environment for advancing themselves and their children than will the underprivileged. The privileged are more likely to perceive the need for change in the educative context; and the less privileged are less likely to understand the nature of the change and, therefore, the need for it. Also, the privileged have the political power and techniques to introduce change in their own communities, whereas the less privileged do not. Finally, there are many more of the less privileged. Politically and logistically, coping with their needs will be more difficult.

Thus, the exceptionally talented or otherwise privileged will continue to find it easier to meet the social and intellectual requirements for remaining in the planning and decision-making elites; for dealing with exceedingly complex social, scientific, and ethical problems; and for exploring and solving them by complex techniques. Those who are not so privileged will tend to become increasingly separated from the program and policy levels of national and private enterprise and from those other aspects of life which are dependent upon sharing the education, values, attitudes, preoccupations, and other characteristics of these elites.

Given the intellectual and operational abilities of the

privileged group and their desire to use them; given
the coming emphasis on leisure activities among the
well-paid, skilled population; given the inability and
lack of motivation in the underprivileged groups to take
on skill-based tasks, it is likely that there will be a growing mutual inclination to let the few look after the many.

The picture we have surveyed is not a tidy or a very
pleasant one. To be sure, we have anticipated improvements in the United States in education and living standards, and in fuller lives for some. But over all, the picture seems depressing. Not that 1984 or a Brave New
World are to be our lot: the society seems too big and
too full of contrary trends and unanticipated consequences for anything so monolithic to be very likely.
But overtones of Orwell and Huxley lurk in much that
we have examined. And combined with these overtones
is a sense that our society is too unwieldy either to provide comfortable assurance that we will avoid 1984 or
to permit a general solution, within our framework of
familiar values and modes of social conduct, to the interlocking problems we have outlined. Our sensed im-
potency, either to preserve the present or to make the
future fulfill our national myth that "progress" lies
ahead, necessarily results in feelings of depression—
even while we realize that those responsible for youth
development may have some favorable impact on the
future.

Also distressing is the nagging prospect that even
though many of us would not like the world described here, it is by no means impossible that those
growing into it and of it, those who are not dispossessed
or unemployed or otherwise "losers," will be at least
as comfortable and content as we are with our world.
After all, many people now live indifferently, apathet-

ically, even happily, with decaying cities, racial inequities, megaton weapons, and the population explosion, as members of the bureaucratic rat race, with their private lives on file, and so on through a catalogue of society's failures which would have depressed a reader of an earlier day.

What, then, is an appropriate philosophy for guiding youth into the kind of world we have speculated on? We cannot know whether there can be a meaningful one, much less what it might be, until we review prevailing philosophies and operations in the light of the plausibilities we have considered. The Appendix outlines a series of questions, deriving from conditions we have speculated about, focused on specific aspects of youth-development issues and operations. These questions, if honestly pursued, should aid in conducting such an exploration.

There are and will be under way a growing variety of exciting and disturbing projects which have the potential for influencing the direction and pace of change. But we must recognize, too, limitations on the rate and scope of changes as a result of the time it takes people and institutions to learn new ideas and new approaches. If we keep a vivid appreciation of the changes tomorrow may hold, and if we keep, too, a sober sense of our limited capacity to influence the trends involved, we ought at least to be able to plan more realistically for youth. As Robert Heilbroner remarks near the end of *The Future as History:*

There are, after all, great traditions of responsibility and social flexibility in America. In them there may yet reside the impetus to seize the historic possibilities before us, and to make those changes which may be necessary if the forces of history are not to sweep over us in an uncontrolled and destructive fashion. But it is useless to hope that this will happen so long as we persist in believing that in the future toward which we are blindly careering everything is "possible," or that we can escape the ultimate responsibility of defining our limits of possibility for ourselves. (1)

In particular, regardless of the great personal pain it will entail, we must explore, more honestly and intensively than most of us ever do, which of the values and goals that we hold dear are appropriate to inculcate in youth for living in tomorrow's world—or for ourselves to live by in planning for and guiding them. Only if we have the candor and courage to do this can we hope to help youth into their world or to live meaningfully in ours.

Reference

1. Heilbroner, Robert L., *The Future as History*. New York: Grove Press, 1961, p. 190.

Appendix

SOME QUESTIONS AND ACTIONS PERTINENT FOR ORIENTING YOUTH-DEVELOPMENT PROGRAMS TO THE PLAUSIBLE FUTURE

1. *What are the implications of these trends for the philosophies of purpose underlying particular youth-development activities?*

If we are moving toward an elitist society, whose obligation is it to accelerate it, whose to obstruct it? If we are going to face skill shortages, which youth-development needs ought to take priority over which others? Which youth-development needs ought to take more or less priority over which other societal needs? If we are moving into a period of turmoil and frustration as well as of accomplishment, what is the proper balance between optimism and cold realism to be conveyed to youth? What is to be the relationship between youth development aimed at fulfillment of the individual and that aimed at the needs of the society? To what extent do the imperatives of youth development, in the light of the future, merit direct involvement by youth-development agencies in the political process at state and local levels? How shall we deal with the possibility that, while we may not like the shape of tomorrow's world, those living in it will find it no less comfortable than today's—possibly more so? When do we fight for and attempt to inculcate values and expectations which seem more in keeping with living productively in tomorrow's world? What kind of civic participation do we teach, if tomorrow's government problems will be dealt with chiefly by a highly trained professionalized group? How do we balance the pressures for technical specialty preparation against the need for more humanistic preparation for meaningful leisure? How do we reconcile present substantive and administrative jurisdictions among youth-development agencies in the light of anticipated problems which would overlap jurisdictions or wipe them out?

2. *Among the various trends and circumstances and their interrelations, which, to a first approximation, are most germane for particular youth-development activities?*

Which factors are most important for those specifically concerned with: college female career training and motivation, slum-level underendowed children, recreation, education in the humanities, school administration, youth retraining in rural areas? What other factors become additionally important when these topics are combined: family mobility? overseas work and play opportunities? urban taxation policies?

3. *In the light of these future conditions, what shifts in emphasis, direction, or resource allocation in youth-development programs merit examination concerning:*
   a. continuing full-scale programs
   b. contemplated full-scale programs
   c. demonstration projects
   d. research programs
   e. public information programs

f. channeling ideals into policy debates
g. affiliations and working arrangements with other organizations
h. short-range planning in all the above
i. long-range planning in all the above.

4. *What knowledge in depth is needed about these future circumstances, and what knowledge is needed about youth, in order to undertake particular youth-development activities in the light of the implications of these circumstances?*

This general question breaks down into questions about:

A. *Available data,* both theory and numbers.

1) What data are already available which take on new implications in the light of these plausible developments?

2) What data are needed which might be collected through existing facilities? For example, what more could be collected through the Census which would gain in utility in association with other information: on the same family, on job-change patterns, dropout rates, career plans, future schooling plans, leisure habits?

3) What data are needed which may require new facilities for collection? And what sorts of facilities would be needed? For example, continuing detailed reliable information *from* industry and government *for* occupational education planners, on anticipated jobs at various times in the future, by numbers, types, wages, and place. . . . Detailed information on lost talent discovered out of school as well as in.

4) What data needs to be collected systematically

through time in order to establish trend lines and benchmarks? For example: specific characteristics of particular socioeconomic groupings of youth about their job expectations, life aspirations, preferred life styles, value commitments, value conflicts, social aversions; styles of expressing frustration and hostility; cynosures; job-change patterns and rates; skills, aptitudes for new types of jobs; for working with different types of people, for working in different types of environments.

5) In what detail must specific data be collected, in order that averaging and sampling will not wash out critical differences between groups, regions, etc., which would reveal significant alternative youth problems and opportunities?

B. *Needed research* to provide understanding and numerical data for applying it.

1) What research is necessary to provide new measures and categories for meaningful and useful data-collecting? For example, what are relevant indices and indicators of social change —rate, direction, site? In youth? In adults?

2) New research problems

a) What new research areas concerning youth will become pressing? How much anxiety is induced by increasing pressures for career preparation, and under what circumstances does it result in opting out? Which occupations suffer? Which gain thereby? Who are the new cynosures for youth groups, and how do they affect the various modes of expression, work aspirations and patterns, leisure activities, values, and view-·

points? How are the standards of the cynosures communicated? How significant are
they for reality training? How useful are
they for preparing for the future? What psychologically and socially valid means can
be devised for providing better-than-equal
opportunities for the underprivileged youth?
How can higher status be provided for low-
status tasks? How can high-status tasks be
reorganized to come within the compass of
low-ability youth? What means can be developed to ease the strain between parents
and adolescents by providing better facilities with which youth can experiment with
autonomy—boarding high schools? greater
opportunities to attend distant colleges?

b) What new research problems will become
urgent about those who most closely mold
and guide youth (including the people de-
liberating on these questions)? What are
the characteristics and distribution of attitudes toward youth problems and opportunities and their relation to beliefs about the
future, among parents, teachers, school administrators, religious leaders, politicians,
school boards, police, and so on and on?
How do these relate to the kinds of opportunities and inhibitions affecting planning,
programs, and youth itself in the light of
anticipated developments? How do these
different groups rank youth problems vis-à-
vis other local and national pressures and
priorities, present and contemplated?

c) What new research areas will be urgent

about the larger context, as exemplified by
the factors attended to in this book? What
are the specific contemplated effects of specific technological developments on youth
life styles and their opportunities to attain or
avoid them? On the expected life styles of
youth when grown to adults? On specific
jobs rather than job categories? What so-
cial-political, national, and international developments most significantly affect youth
behavior and plans? What are the effects
on different youth groups of perceiving a
threatening future? a favorable future?
What factors most influence those expectations? What are the effects, good and bad,
on values, behavior, motives, etc., of the
differentiation between the brilliant and the
average, the favored and the disadvantaged?
How are the effects modified by the degree
to which youth sense the relative perma-
nence of the division as fixed by expected
social trends? To what extent do the changing roles and operating styles of professionals, especially scientists, engineers, and
managers, affect the images of youth as to
the political-ethical nature of the world and,
thereby, the proper conduct for them? What
is their sense of future political potency and
practice and how are their present political
activities affected by the extent to which
they recognize the growing rationalization
and professionalization of government?
What are the costs and benefits of vocational guidance, recreation, retraining, men-

tal health, etc., when specific programs are compared by systems analyses applying advanced economic and behavioral science methods? as functions of specific alternative future conditions? How do major investments in such specific youth-development areas compare, in terms of national costs and benefits, with allocations of funds, skills, equipment, and plant to other needs? What measures of cost and benefit are most useful for legislative purposes? What humanitarian alternatives can be imagined which may give better ratios of costs to benefits for the direct recipients and for the rest of the nation?

d) What new research areas become pressing about institutional arrangements facilitating change in and responsiveness to youth problems and opportunities? For example, systems analyses directed to the invention of administrative and organizational arrangements that are keyed to meeting changing conditions as these relate to their ostensible youth-development purposes. Invention of means for overcoming internal resistance to disruption of vested interests in these organizations. Invention of new environments for coping with change and the new problems and opportunities it presents, such as work-learn-play camps, family-as-a-unit retraining facilities, occupational status upgrading or downgrading methods, work-and-travel mobility encouragers. Means for providing "second chances" for "late bloomers" or those who want to change careers and have special competences. Redistribution and enlargement of factors affecting school prestige and status. Developing curricula and environment which encourage the fullest personal development and social utility of the mentally underendowed.

C. *Evaluation*

What can be learned from present programs that is not now being learned concerning their adequacy to deal with specific futures?

5. *How can the capacity be institutionalized to alter programs in the light of anticipated, but not proven, developments and to revise these as time goes on?*

A. A communication network between youth development planners and permanent advisory groups.

B. A within-organization capability of repeating and implementing on a continuing basis the steps outlined above.

A CONTINUING ADVISORY GROUP
FOR RE-EVALUATING
AND EXTENDING SPECULATIONS
ON IMPORTANT FUTURE TRENDS

In the very nature of this book, it should be updated as we move into the future. Not only will some speculations prove misleading in direction or import, but special events will introduce unforeseeable perturbations. Indeed, an attempted forecast may, as often happens in the economic realm, alter the future by its very presence. Also, as data of the sort suggested in the

above outline accumulate, the ability to make more subtle and integrated speculations about the long term probably will improve. Finally, if the present book succeeds in stimulating reviews of and revisions in present
programs and the establishment of new ones, it would
be most useful to take advantage of this accomplishment by supplying planning, research, and action groups
with newer information that would allow them to further
refine their activities. Since the costs in money and
skilled resources will increase for programs which deal
with the problems and opportunities of youth, any methods which allow a more efficient allocation of effort
should be most desirable. Systematic review of the anticipated future is such a method.

A small work group using approach and methods similar to those utilized in the preparation of this book
would offer a simple and effective means for monitoring
the future. This group should consist of between seven
and eleven people, in order to ensure both variety of
viewpoint and good range of competences and yet ensure continuity of discussion and sufficient confronta-
tion. An incisive, but reasonably permissive, chairman
who will pursue arguments and insist on confrontations
would be a prerequisite. Also prerequisite would be
some staff assistance to prepare working papers, to insure that all participants come to the conferences familiar with presumably significant developments in ideas
and events, and to prepare summary papers. Group
membership probably would benefit from continuity:
enough fresh blood would be introduced over time by
the natural cycle of events for professional people. If
desirable, special resource participants could be invited
for particular purposes at particular meetings.

It would be highly desirable to have participating two

bright, knowledgeable college students, one of each sex. They would hardly represent the range of youth attitudes and understanding: the very fact that they would be chosen for their capacity to contribute to such proceedings would mean they did not represent the typical college student. Nevertheless, it would be most salutary to have their reactions to adult speculations about trends in youth itself.

The group should meet once annually for two to four consecutive days, away from distractions and interruptions. Also present as observers and resource people, and also able to "participate" out of session, should be representatives from the sponsoring agency. Also, part of the deliberations of the group ought to be devoted to trends and circumstances that the sponsoring agency itself anticipates and feels may be important. It is especially important that this effort not become isolated from those who sponsor it: there is no quicker or surer way to have the activity become mere ritual and the results end up on the shelf. Futhermore, it will be impossible to establish a continuing group if they feel their time is thus wasted.

Although the deliberations of the group could be used exclusively by the sponsor, they would be much more valuable if summaries were distributed to those youth-development planning organizations that would benefit from them. If this course were followed it would also be highly worth while to set up a feedback system to learn: a) the extent to which the agencies do, in fact, incorporate these speculations into their plans and revisions of plans; and b) what further information they need to do so. In this way the sponsoring agency would itself gain important insights for planning and supporting additional research, demonstration programs, and data collection. If these recommendations are followed, the chances will be good indeed that today's planning for youth development will be more congruent with—and will have more influence on—tomorrow's world.

INDEX

ABOUT THE AUTHOR

DONALD N. MICHAEL, who was born in Chicago in 1923, is a social psychologist with a background in the physical sciences. He was educated at Harvard University and the University of Chicago, and after receiving his Ph.D. from Harvard, taught at Boston University. As a researcher and advisor, Dr. Michael has worked with a number of government and scientific agencies, including the Joint Chiefs of Staff, the National Science Foundation, and UNESCO. He is presently Chairman of the Subcommittee on Long-Range Problems of Peace and War of the Society for the Psychological Study of Social Issues, Chairman of the American Psychological Association's Committee on Cybernation, and a member of the Technical Committee on Law and Sociology of the American Institute of Aeronautics and Astronautics.

Dr. Michael has published many professional papers, essays, and reports on the social and psychological challenges produced by a rapidly changing technology. Among these are the Brookings Institution publication, *Proposed Studies on the Implications of Peaceful Space Activities for Human Affairs*, and *Cybernation: The Silent Conquest*, published by the Fund for the Republic's Center for the Study of Democratic Institutions at Santa Barbara. He is at present a Resident Fellow of the Institute for Policy Studies in Washington, D.C.